Charles William Gedney

Angling Holidays

In Pursuit of Salmon, Trout and Pike

Charles William Gedney

Angling Holidays
In Pursuit of Salmon, Trout and Pike

ISBN/EAN: 9783337143367

Printed in Europe, USA, Canada, Australia, Japan

Cover: Foto ©Andreas Hilbeck / pixelio.de

More available books at **www.hansebooks.com**

ANGLING HOLIDAYS.

IN PURSUIT OF

SALMON, TROUT AND PIKE,

—BY—

C. W. GEDNEY.

FIRST EDITION.

"TELEGRAPH" PRINTING WORKS, BROMLEY, KENT.

1896.

INDEX TO CHAPTERS.

	Page
DOVEDALE TROUT AND TRENT SALMON	5
ON THE ATLANTIC COAST	12
SOME IRISH ADVENTURES AND EXPERIENCES	19
DRY FLY FISHING AND OTHER THINGS	29
GWEEDORE, CO. DONEGAL	38
AUTUMN NORFOLK TROUTING	50
THE BANN AT COLERAINE	56
THE BANN AT KILREA	59
THE RIVER SHANNON	75
THE RIVER DARENTH	81
MAY-FLY ON DARENTH	88
LAST DAY ON DARENTH	111
THE MOY AT BALLINA	116
LAKE VYRNWY	122
THE RIVER BUSH AT BUSHMILLS	134
AUTUMN PIKE FISHING	140
THE WILTSHIRE AVON	147
THE USK, MONMOUTHSH'RE	149
KILLALOE ON SHANNON	154
GALWAY AND BALLANAHINCH	157
WESTPORT, CO. MAYO	161
WINCHESTER OLD BARGE	162
CANTERBURY STOUR	165
ANGLING HOLIDAYS IN SCOTLAND	167

LIST OF ILLUSTRATIONS.

	Page
ENTRANCE OF DOVEDALE	4
IN DOVEDALE—THE POOL	7
DOVEDALE—NEAR THE STRAITS	9
DONEGAL—THE POISONED GLEN	38
GWEEDORE—THE SALMON LEAP	40
GWEEDORE LOUGH	44
THE BANN AT COLERAINE	56
THE "CUTTS" AT COLERAINE	58
THE BANN ABOVE COLERAINE	59
THE BANN AT KILREA—PORTNA WEIR	62
THE BANN AT KILREA	69
THE SHANNON—THE FERRY	75
THE SHANNON RAPIDS	78
SHANNON—DOONA'S FALLS	80
THE DARENTH—EYNSFORD POOL	81
DARENTH—THE AUTHOR AT WORK	88
THE CLUB COTTAGE ON DARENTH	91
EYNSFORD CHUMS	95
DARENTH AT EYNSFORD—SPRATT'S POOL	106
RIVER MOY—THE GAS WORK'S CAST	116
THE ASH TREE CAST—RIVER MOY	118
LAKE VYRNWY	122
RIVER BUSH AT BUSHMILLS	134
BUSHMILLS—THE FALLS	138
THE WILTSHIRE AVON	147
THE USK AT ABERGAVENNY	149
KILLALOE ON SHANNON	154
SHANNON AT KILLALOE	156
GALWAY BRIDGE	157
GALWAY SALMON FISHERY	158
CLIFDEN CO. GALWAY	159
BALLINAHINCH, CO. GALWAY	160
WESTPORT, CO. MAYO	161
WINCHESTER, THE OLD BARGE	162
THE ITCHEN—LORD NORTHBROOK'S FISHERY	164
CANTERBURY STOUR	166
LOCH LOMOND	167
LOCH KATRINE	168
LOCH LEVEN, ARGYLESHIRE	169
LOCH LEVEN IN GLENCOE	170
LOCH LEVEN AND PASS OF GLENCOE	171
LOCH EARN	172
LOCH TAY	173
RIVER DOCHART	175
LOCH AWE	176
THE RIVER ORCHY	177
PASS OF BRANDER	178

PREFACE.

It is with some misgiving that I have yielded to the pressure put upon me by brother fishermen, and thus added one more to the already long catalogue of angling books. But this is not a fishing book of the orthodox pattern; it is a gossipy record of a sportsman's experiences. If there appears an absence of connection between some of the chapters, let me explain that many of them were written as letters at various periods, to beguile the lonely evenings of a solitary angler in remote fishing quarters. These articles were never designed for publication in book form, but the lovers of all that pertains to angling will, none the less, I hope, find some entertainment in their perusal. A few of them have previously appeared—in substance—in the "Illustrated Sporting and Dramatic News," and my thanks are due to the courtesy of the proprietor of that journal for his consent to their reproduction. Wherever I could do so, I have given full and accurate details of the places fished, and how the fishing is obtainable; but this has not been possible in the case of private waters. It has also been necessary to use fictitious names, in a good many instances, in order to disguise the identity of individuals.

With these brief words of explanation and introduction, I commend "Angling Holidays" to the perusal of all true disciples of Isaac Walton.

C. W. G.

Bromley, Kent, 1896.

THE ENTRANCE OF DOVEDALE.

From photo by R. Bull, Ashbourne.

DOVEDALE TROUT AND TRENT SALMON.

I have spent several very delightful angling holidays in Dovedale, and for early spring trout fishing I know of no place more enjoyable. Later on in the season, the fierce midsummer sun pouring down into the dale—without a breath of wind to temper its rays—is rather too much of a good thing. My first trout from the Dove was taken from the stepping-stones shown in our illustration of the "Entrance of Dovedale." The river can there be crossed by a series of stones, which form a little cascade. I was standing upon these stepping-stones, admiring the vista of the opening dale before me, and my cast dragged neglected in the stream behind me. My day-dream was broken by a heavy "rug," and I found, to my amazement, that a pound trout had "yanked on," as they say in the States. This was polite on the part of the Dove trout to thus come to net uninvited, but I did not find any more of them so complaisant. The Dove is a somewhat slow-running river, the water being held back by small artificial weirs at short intervals, and these obstructions make some pretty little cascades. In the runs below these falls most of the anglers seek their sport, but I did better upon the deep glassy "flats" at the entrance of the dale with a floating fly. The May fly was just coming on when I arrived at the old Isaac Walton Hotel, and before many days it was up in teeming thousands, that fairly enveloped the angler. I never saw such a rise of May fly in my life, either before or since, and it lasted during a period of ten days. The natives and visitors fished in orthodox fashion, with light 12ft. bamboo rods and fine Stewart tackle. A small basket, containing female May fly, strapped round the waist, and two of these flies were impaled, one above the other, on the hooks. This class of fishing was all done in the fast water beneath the cascades, and anything more murderous I never saw. I preferred to float an alder, of large size, on the deep slow-running water, where I got some very handsome fish, including two splendid grayling close on 2lb. apiece. These fish were both dimpling at the opposite side to the one I was fishing, and they were moving about some blades of grass which hung into the stream. It was a long cast for a wee 10ft. rod but I ultimately got the alder across on to the bank, and worked it gently down on to the water. There it remained, until the sagging line sunk it, and as the fly went under something moved beneath it, and I struck. Then the fun began, for I was fast in a big fish, which fought backwards, in jerks, down stream, and skittered round in quite a different manner to a trout. When, finally, he came to net, I found this big grayling had a round turn of the cast around his body, and the alder firmly fixed in the corner of his mouth. It was a grand fish of fully 2lb. weight, but I had a horrible misgiving that grayling were out of season. Putting him into my landing net, and fixing the net in the water, with the net handle driven into the bank, I made my way up to the cascade above in search of information. The man fishing there heard my story and my doubts, and he assured me, most emphatically, that grayling were out of season, and foreshadowed my appearance at Ashbourne Petty Sessions. The result was that I sadly retraced my steps, and still more sadly returned "Thymallus" to his native element. Then the keeper came along, and I told him what had happened. "You don't mean to say you put the fish back?" he asked, in astonishment. I assured him I had done so, and then he told me that the close time for grayling had been over for a week! This was very galling, and the more so as my experiences of two-pound graylings were then very limited. But I set to work again on those bank feeders, and within a dozen feet of where the other fish was hooked I got another under precisely similar circumstances. And, what was still more curious, this fish wound himself round the cast precisely in the same manner as the first had done. They were the counterparts of each

IN DOVEDALE.—THE POOL.
From photo by R. Bull, Ashbourne.

other, but they did not both share the same fate—the second grayling went into my basket! That man on whose advice I returned the first fish had a bad ten minutes when we met in the smoking-room that evening.

In the middle reach of the river, which is shown in our second illustration, I had some very pretty fishing with an oak fly—a gaudy, waspish-coloured artificial. I spotted a nice little colony of medium-sized trout feeding beneath a stunted overhanging oak tree, which was swarming with the flies which take the name of the tree they feed on. I had not got the artificial, for they are unknown in our southern streams, but I doubled back to a local man, lower down stream, and he gave me what I wanted. Three brace of trout were taken with these oak flies out of a very short length of water, and a very nice little bit of fishing it was. At the upper end of the dale, shown in our third illustration, the water was too low for sport, but the beauty of the place amply compensated us for exploring it.

Bird life in Dovedale is very interesting, and the habits and customs of the water ousel especially interested me. They are wonderfully tame and confiding, are these ousels of the Derbyshire dales, and we watched them as they walked under water, in search of snails and caddis flies. Some persons say these birds eat trout spawn, but I have never seen any evidence in support of the charge. Even if it was true, I would not lose these pretty companions of the angler for the sake of a few trout.

Have you ever had the good fortune to surprise a brood of young sandpipers, or summer snipe? If you have not, then there is something still worth living for—presuming that you care anything for the curiosities of natural history. Unhappily the bulk of mankind know little and care less for such things, I fear, but to those who take delight in matters relating to minute natural history, nothing could be more delightful than to come suddenly upon Mother Sandpiper and her brood of little ones. It has not been my good fortune to do it often, but on this occasion, in Dovedale, I passed round a big rock and saw Mrs. S. and her family preening themselves in the sunshine. There was an electrical jump of the whole party in opposite directions, and they disappeared as if by magic, although they never took flight, and there was not a bush or bit of cover near them. No one, except those whose eyes have been trained by minute natural history study, would have discovered those newly-hatched youngsters. They were lying, apparently dead, amongst the stones, motionless, with closed eyes, and my companion could scarcely be made to see them, even when they were pointed out to him!

An old lady, at whose cottage we told a tale of woe of parched and famished fishermen, offered us of her scanty sustenance. But the solids took the shape of sticky tarts, and the liquid was "nettle tea"! She assured me that this beverage possessed wonderful medicinal properties, that its recuperative powers upon a jaded and exhausted frame were magical. I took one sip of the decoction, and found it the most satisfying liquor I ever tasted in my life, and next to Chinese Samsau I should recommend it for nastiness. My chum threw his lot out of the window, behind the poor old dame's back, and praised it mightily to her face. Declared it reminded him of his boyhood, in the country, when his dear old mother used to make it, and finally got our hostess to give him a recipe for brewing this vile decoction! She was greatly flattered by his praise, and finally insisted upon putting a bottle of the stuff into his fishing bag to take home with him.

In the Islam length of the River Manifold, which runs at the bottom of the grounds attached to the Isaac Walton Hotel, there is excellent fishing for both trout and grayling. It is private water, attached to Islam Hall, and a little lower down this stream becomes merged into the Dove, which in turn empties itself into the Trent. This Manifold River is a mole for a portion of its length, and there are two distinct underground channels through which it flows. I had a few days' good sport on the Manifold, but killed more grayling than trout, and I was much interested in the way in which "Thymallus" took the fly. Casting an alder on the surface of a deep pool, in which the shadowy forms of

DOVEDALE – NEAR THE STRAITS.

From photo by R. Bull, Ashbourne.

the grayling could be seen three feet below, a fish would shoot up with a rush, seize the fly, and drop backwards to the bottom.

At the end of a very enjoyable holiday I broke my homeward journey at Derby, intending only to spend the night there.

We were enjoying a post-prandial cigar in the smoking-room of the Midland Hotel, and amongst the company were two local anglers, who spoke in glowing terms of the resources of the river Trent. I expressed some incredulity about the salmon fishing in a river so polluted as the Trent, and these two gentlemen made a dead set at me to come with them on the morrow and give the river a trial. In vain I pleaded that the tackle with me was limited to the outfit of a dry-fly trout fisherman. They would take no denial, and so I yielded to their importunities and agreed to join them. They fitted me up with a 15 ft. double-handed, whippy trout rod and a Nottingham reel, with 200 yards of twisted flax, about the same thickness as a fine trout line! Of all the unmanageable things in the hands of an inexperienced person, commend me to a Nottingham reel! My experiences with these erratic machines had been very limited, and I loved not the rig-out thus generously lent me; but I was in for it, and therefore made the best of the situation. Within a short railway ride of Derby we got fishing tickets at a quaint little village hostelry, and paid for these permits one shilling each. My shillingsworth was signed "William Cooper," and it gave me the right to fish "Mr. Smith's and Mr. Vicker's water," and it also informed me, in a footnote, that "Parties breaking fences, or leaving gates open, will be discharged." I do not purposely omit the name of the village where these permits were issued—in fact I forget it. Across a couple of fields, and we found ourselves upon the banks of the beery Trent, and along the said banks were disposed at intervals some fifteen anglers—worming for salmon. Within sight, up stream, were some of the big breweries whose refuse pollutes this stream, and sends it down discoloured and frothy, suggestive of "half-and-half." The Trent at this point was about a hundred yards wide, and we fished from a steep bank, some eight or nine feet above the level of the water. After vainly struggling to attain to the "Nottingham style"—which all the local men adopted—I gave it up in despair, and also abandoned the two huge "maiden" worms in favour of a Devon minnow. But the local's style of fishing interested me greatly. With heavily-weighted lines and large tapered floats, they turned their backs to the water, and swinging their baits to and fro, to obtain the necessary momentum, they suddenly wheeled round and sent their baited hooks flying out to great distances, with a delicacy and precision which astonished me. This was the style of fishing adopted in the deep pools, the angler following his float down some distance and then returning to the old spot and repeating the process. At the tail of this deep pool the water shallowed, and there a couple of men fished worm with a heavy ledger lead, one of the men thus capturing a handsome 3lb. trout. It was all strange to me, for, whatever may be my piscatorial sins, I have never yet caught a salmon with a worm! Going up to the head of the deep pool, which was said to hold several big fish, I span diligently, in the Thames style, but the difficulties incidental to doing this with a whippy fly rod will commend themselves to all practical anglers. The day began to draw to a close, no one had yet taken a salmon, and the prospects of a blank were beginning to depress us all. The locals were greatly interested in my style of casting, and the two men below me invited me to go down over their water. In doing so I got a heavy pull, and found myself fast in a big fish. All the anglers gave up fishing, and gathered round me in a crowd, and I doubt if I ever played a fish so badly in my life. That wretched Nottingham reel nearly drove me frantic, for I knew little or nothing of the mysteries of "skidding" with my finger, as practised by those experts who swear by these crazy machines. With a crowd round me, all proffering advice, and several men importuning me to hand them the rod, the experience was by no means a pleasant one. The fish had got over to the opposite bank, and resolutely refused to do anything except run up and down under its friendly shelter. Eventually an angler on that side good-naturedly came up, and beating the water with his net, drove the fish out into mid-stream. By this time I had given up all attempts to play the fish from the winch, and coiled the line at my feet as I got it in—to the great horror of the spectators. "Stand back and give me room," was my only rejoinder to their expostulations, and presently I got my fish well in hand, giving him all the "butt" that the rod was capable of. The salmon was now close to the surface, and occasionally broke the water savagely with his tail, showing that he was nearly done, and presently he rolled over, showing us, for the first time, what a handsome fish he was. Barring accidents, his capture now was only a question of time; but how to get him out was the problem, for the coil of line made it quite impossible to take him down to the low bank a hundred yards below. We fought it out where I hooked him, and a man lying down, with two others holding his legs, gaffed the fish, and he was quickly on the grass—a handsome salmon weighing $22\frac{1}{4}$lb. Thus ended my first and last experiences of fishing in the Trent.

ON THE ATLANTIC COAST.

I am the guest of a local magnate, on the banks of an Irish salmon river. Let us call our host the General, and let us, also, congratulate ourselves that a pressing engagement prevents him fishing this morning. We will try his favourite pool, which is the most likely place to yield a salmon in the present low state of the water. A small fly, with gold tinsel body, wings and tail of golden pheasant toppings and tippets, and legs of blue chatterer—boasting the appropriate name of Lord Randolph—such a fly should lure one of those sulky beggars to destruction if anything will; so, let us start with Randy. Deftly the glittering morsel goes thirty yards across the pool, and falls straight and true, with a tight line, giving little chance of a miss, should "Salmo salar" accept the invitation to lunch. A shelving bank, which shallows the tail end of the pool, is the usual "catch," but the fly passes the magic spot, and the cast is repeated with varying lengths of line until presently there is a boil in the water, a huge blue back shows itself, followed by a nine-inch tail, and the screaming winch proclaims the fact that the fight has begun. With a mighty rush, the big fish takes off line at greased lightning speed, and, making for some shallows, wallows over them into deep water beyond, followed by the angler, slipping and stumbling over boulders, with an utter disregard of broken shins. Panting, and almost exhausted, the quarry is overtaken, but he declines to discuss the matter at such close quarters, and once more there is a furious rush up stream, with more obstacle racing, floundering and blundering, whilst Paddy yells, "Hould 'im up, yer honor! hould 'im up! or by the holy Saints he'll cut ye on the shallers!" He does nothing of the kind, but, regaining his old ground, takes to somersault and vaulting, showing himself to be a grand twenty pounder. Doggedly he bores to the bottom and "sniggers" the line in a fashion which nearly always indicates an insecure hold on the part of the hook. With another wild dash, he goes tearing the line out—sixty, seventy, eighty yards go off, as he hugs the opposite bank, and there is a horrid rock in the river, only thirty yards below him. If once he gets beyond it, he will trump my trick, and win the game. Butt him all I dare, he holds on his course; the rod creaks beneath the heavy strain to no purpose, and in another minute he is behind the snag, gets a dead pull, and the line comes back —the hook has drawn! There are some griefs too deep and sacred to be laid bare to the public gaze; and the veil is drawn over the utter desolation of a man who lost in this way the only big salmon that had rewarded three weeks of incessant labour!

For three weeks we have been getting either south or westerly gales in Ireland, accompanied by occasional smart showers, and a leaden sky. One or two bright days only have we had, and these have occurred when the wind chopped round to the north-east; but the old Cornish fisherman's proverb, "When the wind goes round agin' the sun, don't pay no heed, for back she'll come," proved true—back "she" did come. But the fishing has been fairly good, notwithstanding the salmon's objection to rise to a fly if there is "water over them." That is the way in which Mike describes the presence of rain clouds overhead. He played a mean trick one day this week on a jealous angler. This fisherman set a bank line at a spot reputed to be the haunt of one of those fabulous giant pike, which are said to exist in almost every bit of water in this watery island. Our old friend had been beguiled by his attendant—Mike's rival—into having a go for the capture of this mythical monster, and Mike having induced me to shoot him a comorant—under the pretence of wanting some feathers for fly-dressing—he, quite unbeknown to me, attached the bird to the bank line of the aforesaid angler. The bait was thrust down the bird's throat, and the hooks were so artistically fixed, that the owner was imposed upon, and he has sent the bird to be stuffed as a memento of a very remarkable capture! I hope he won't see this confession, but should he do so, I trust that he will acquit me of any knowledge of the affair, until a week after it occurred, when the hoax was common talk amongst "the boys," and I became aware of it by being asked whether I had shot the bird for Mike. My jealous neighbour has had a bad time of it, for he has seen a twenty-eight pounder killed under his very nose this week, and also seen the opposition boat going home with two, three, and four fish each evening, while his total score for the week has been one poor little grilse, and that taken with a trailing spoon! No wonder he is sour, because you can forgive a man anything else in the world except catching more fish than you do. By the way, my faithful henchman cooked me a fish dinner the other day in a fashion which must be at once the oldest—and it certainly is one of the best—known methods of roasting. Having excavated a round hole in the earth, and paved it with pieces of rock, a turf fire is lighted on the stones, and others were arranged around like a grotto to get heated as the fire burnt up. Whilst the fire was going on, a couple of handsome trout, of 1lb. and 2lbs. respectively, were carefully rolled up separately in well-buttered paper. The oven being hot enough, the red-hot embers were taken off the stones, and the trout placed upon them. Other hot stones were placed artistically round the fish—without pressing on them—the burning embers of peat were placed around the cairn, and we went away to catch more fish whilst the cooking was in progress. A flight of teal comes swishing past us as we push off from our "dissolute island," as Mike called it, and a charge of No. 5, from the "full choke," stopped the flight of one of the travellers. He was only winged, however, and by the time he had been bagged shouts from the cook announced that the meal was ready. And what a feast for a king it was! Those trout were simply done to perfection, and when eaten with oaten scones and butter, washed down with Guiness's bottled stout, he would be a dainty man who, after a hard morning's fishing, from 7 to 12, did not do ample justice to such a feast. Mike has been fed upon trout, salmon, and eels all his life, and he, therefore, preferred to fall back upon our potted wares. First he tackled a tin of sardines, and having disposed of the whole lot satisfactorily, I passed him over a pot of Crosse and Blackwell's highly-seasoned potted game. He toyed with this a bit at first, not being quite sure of his ground, but eventually, to my amazement, I found that he had raked out the contents into a plate, and was disposing of it in "chunks" about the size of small potatoes. He had by this time eaten about two pounds of bread, but he still looked wistfully at the provision basket, and I, therefore, gave him another course. This time it was an oaten scone of 1lb. and four hard boiled eggs, two of them being turkey's, and his face expanded with a grin so broad that it made his ears hang down. Mike having finally exhausted the provisions, without having exhausted his appetite, went to the water's edge and, lying down, put his face in the river, and took a long drink by way of topping up his meal. My faithful henchman, however, is by no means a teetotaller, in fact, he is very frequently much the reverse— in fact, he is an ether drinker. "You are an awful thirsty man," said I to him, at that feast above referred to, and I added, "You must surely have been made of some very dry materials." "Bedad!" he exclaimed, "But your honor's right, 'tis not me own fault at all; me poor old mother was a Cork woman!" As I have already said, Pat was an ether drinker, and, thanks to his assistance, I have been able to find out many interesting details as to the prevalence and extent of the use of this pernicious spirit. Sixpennyworth of ether will go further—that is, produce more intoxication —than half-a-crown's worth of whisky. "But it gives you bad heads," Mike assured me, on the "days after." The villages in the North of Ireland are plentifully supplied with ether by wholesale dealers, and I was given the name of a man in an adjacent town who carries on an extensive trade in this spirit. It is largely used in the adulteration of whisky by retail dealers, and those accustomed to its peculiar flavour do not detect its presence in the adulterated article; in fact, they like it. When this subject was mooted in the House of Commons some time ago the Government promised to immediately adopt measures to suppress this traffic, but nothing has been done, and the stuff is openly sold, without restriction, in the village where I am located. Discussing the subject the other evening with one of the leading Government officials in Ulster, he said he had little doubt that this use of ether as an intoxicant was doing an immense amount of injury, and that it ought to be rigorously suppressed. In his opinion, the increase of insanity was attributable to the drinking of ether. On Wednesday I found myself in proximity to a market town, and therefore devoted a couple of hours to pricing some of the goods. All kinds of live stock were very cheap, including horses, of which there was an unlimited supply, mostly youngsters. Farmers' wives were selling new laid eggs at 8d. per dozen, and fowls ranged from 7d. to 9d. each, according to size and condition. Geese fetched from 1s. 6d. to 2s., and mutton was selling at 7d. to 8d. per lb. for the prime joints, whilst pork went at 5d. and 6d. per lb. It sounds all right to hear of fowls at 7d. each, but they are like the cows, poor little things, and a hungry man could eat two of them for a meal—the chicken, I mean, not the cows. Of an Irishman's fowls you might with truth say:—

> "Your salmon are so fat and red,
> Your chicken are so thin and blue;
> 'Tis plain to see which God has fed,
> And which was fed by you."

Everywhere one hears the same bitter complaints as to the decline of the potato crop in Ireland. I discussed the subject with a lot of farmers, and they were unanimously of opinion that potatoes had been going back, as a crop in Ireland, for many years, and that every season they got worse, and the disease became greater. One old man closed the discussion by saying, "I can mind when 'taties was sixpence a bushel of three stone, and this year I paid 5s. a bushel for seed!" The truth is, that on these small holdings the same ground is cropped with potatoes, year after year with the same old seed, until the ground sickens for the want of change, and the tuber deteriorates from the same cause.

As this is a question of national importance, which vitally affects the subsistence of the poorer people of Ireland, something ought to be done to assist them in the matter. Although the north-western section of Ireland, where I am located, is exposed to the full fury of the Atlantic gales, and catches every capful of rain which collects in that watery waste, the climate here is much less trying to vegetation than in England. Take last winter as a case in point. The Siberian winter which visited England, and froze our water pipes six feet below the ground for three months, never touched Ireland! " There were one or two light frosts, but nothing more," said my host, when I asked how he got over the winter of 1895. Amongst some of the resident gentry in this part of Ireland cock fighting is still a common so-called sport. The police take no notice of the matter; the official classes, which constitute the bulk of the residents "who toil not, neither do they spin," being apparently exempt from that rigorous enforcement of "law and order." As some of these cock fighters are amongst my personal friends, I feel constrained not to make full use of the information in my possession. But this much I can say, that cock fights for high stakes are common, and that these fights are attended by large gatherings of magistrates, officers, and Government officials.

Of all the strange creatures that furnish food for man, commend me to the salmon; and of all the uncertain, but glorious, sports there is none that equals salmon fishing. In spite of all the books and learned essays that have been written upon the subject of how to catch him Mr. "Salmo Salar" is as difficult of capture and as full of whims and caprices, which we cannot overcome, as he was before so much ink and learning had been devoted to his destruction. All their actions are governed by certain laws of nature which have yet to be understood by man, but that which is true of a salmon in one river will by no means be equally true of a similar fish in another river. To illustrate my meaning I will explain what occurred here last Monday.

There had been a large number of salmon showing on a rocky shallow on the lower portion of the water I am fishing, and the spot had been coveted by the jealous angler above referred to for the past fortnight. But the fish would not take his flies, although he plied them with patterns of every shade, and with every lure that he could think of. On Monday the wind chopped from west to south, and my man Pat remarked, "If this wind holds the night, we'll have all the fish up in our pool the morn." The distance between the two points is about three miles, and Pat was unable to offer any other explanation of his prophesy than the fact that the fish always came from the lower to the upper pools if the south wind lasted twelve hours. The wind held, and we saw our sour old rival race off to secure his pool long before we had breakfasted! Sure enough the fish had come up, and here they were in scores, at our very door, and in the first hour's fishing we had killed one splendid clean fish, fresh from the sea, and played and lost two others. Then they went off the fly, and resolutely refused to be further tempted by the brilliantly-tinted combination of fur, feathers, and tinsel with which we sought to beguile them. Spoons of silver, and spoons of gold, were spun in vain over them, and we even resorted to prawns, with the same negative results, and thus the afternoon wore away, the fish meanwhile rising around us. Pat was at his wits end, working and swearing his hardest, whilst Mike exasperated both master and man by incessantly suggesting that, maybe, they would take things that had already been tried in vain. Finally we gave up in despair, and went away to another cast higher up. Here the same bad luck attended us, for we only got one small fish, and lost two big fellows in succession. We gave up at five o'clock, and on our way down found a friend of mine in the pool we had left vacant. He had killed four fish, and was playing his fifth, which he also landed, and he took them all with a silver minnow. The jealous angler got nothing.

SOME IRISH ADVENTURES AND EXPERIENCES.

What a terrible time we have had of it in Ireland since the foregoing chapter was written. Gales of wind and deluges of rain have followed each other with only short intervals of a few hours between, and the rivers have been turned into raging torrents. For seven successive days angling had—up to Saturday—been quite out of the question, when a neighbour of mine beguiled me into accompanying him to a mountain-fed river from which the flood runs off in a few hours, and the fishing is good in the clearing water. After a week's enforced idleness the prospect of sport was pleasant, as was the fifteen-mile drive, in the keen morning air, on my friend's shooting car. We found the river had been over its banks, but the water had now fallen to a reasonable level—although still too high—and no time was lost in getting a shelter for the horse and seeking the services of some attendant gossoon to carry our gaff and lunch. But no such gossoon could we find, and we discussed the situation seriously. My friend's car driver was a veritable Handy Andy—rejoicing in the name of Larry—and the idea of taking him with us and sending him back for the car when the day's work was done appeared to me to be the most sensible course to adopt, and I said so. "Ah!" replied my friend, "that would be all very well if we had anyone else; but you don't know Larry or you wouldn't suggest it. No; we must carry our packs and let him pick us up at the footbridge eight miles lower down in the evening." This was so arranged, and many and explicit were the details given to Larry to start at half-past four and follow the road straight down till he came to a bridge, and there await our coming. Away we went, with light hearts, and, with true Irish courtesy, my friend insisted upon my taking the lead—he would rather go home

without wetting a fly than have it otherwise. So off we
went, over the soddened boggy land, from which but a few
hours before the flood had subsided, and it was heavy going
I do assure you. The first two miles of water was all fishable and fish it we did, without moving a fin; then we
changed our flies, mopped ourselves, and admired each
other's bog-besmeared legs—truth to tell, we honoured the
toast of "Health to men and death to fishes." Then we
went at it again, and floundered on, flogging the water with
redoubled energy, and spiritually inspired anticipations!
Another mile was thus passed, when a famous "carry" was
reached, my friend assuring me that if we failed to score in
this pool the prospects of a blank day were very much
against us. But we did score—as I had good reason
to repent hereafter—a twelve pounder accepted my line
of invitation to lunch, without a moment's hesitation.
He made a poor fight of it, as I was somewhat hard on
him; being anxious not to disturb the lower end of
the pool. Having grassed our first salmon, we lit our
pipes, and wrangled as to whether I should fish the remainder of the pool, and let my host follow me, or
whether he should first go over the water, as yet undisturbed. My host was about the most obstinate of his
countrymen that I ever met, and as he was moreover
deaf to every argument, I went over the water first, in order
to gratify his Quixotic courtesy towards a guest. Having
fished it about as carelessly and badly as possible, I took a
seat, relit my pipe, and waited my friend's arrival. He
literally searched every inch of the water, and excited my
admiration by the patient manner in which he tried every
eddy, swirl, and resting place wherein an upward bound
fish might halt to take breath. From my elevated position
the flies were easily watched as they danced with life-like
motion, and when the angler was on the point of lifting
them a splendid fish rose and seized the dropper. There was
a grand fight, but the result was—bar accidents—never in
doubt, and in a short quarter of an hour a well-fed, but
somewhat red, seventeen pounder received his quietus by
being ignominiously thumped on the head with a lump of

rock. We slung our fish, head and tail after a brief rest, and hung them across our shoulders, then we squelched on, through the sponge-like sodden ground, and followed the snake-like windings of that river for a few more miles without anything to vary the monotony except the difficulty of getting across intervening ditches, clambering over stone walls, and forcing oneself through blackthorn hedges. How we did enjoy ourselves! But this kind of thing is very satisfying, and when we had kept it up 'till between two and three o'clock—after five hours' tramping—it was carried unanimously that all the edibles and drinkables in our fishing bags should be disposed of. We did justice to the frugal fare, and wished there had been more of it; we did ditto by our flasks, and expressed our mutual disgust at the small capacity of those "wretched things"; then we had another pipe. How far was it to the bridge? Oh! about another four miles, if we followed the windings of the river, and that was the best way. I began to think that twelve pounder was not such a good-looking fish as he appeared to be when first I slung him round my neck. Four miles more, floundering over boggy ground, carrying that fish, with a salmon rod and gaff, and a fishing bag to boot, was not a pleasant prospect, but it had to be done, so on we went. Here and there, at likely pools I had a few casts, more for the sake of a rest than anything else, and finally, after two hours' hard plodding, we reached our trysting place, the footbridge across the river. I was fairly done up, and my host, a wiry fellow, sank down by the roadside, under the load of his seventeen pounder and a big rod, and groaned out "Where is that blackguard Larry, and the car?" Where, indeed; we were too much pumped out to trouble much at first—it was barely five o'clock—but soon it began to spit with rain, and an ominous black cloud spread its mantle across the sky, and at half-past five it was almost dark, and the rain coming down pretty smartly. Still no signs of Larry and his car! We were sixteen miles from home and the nearest village was ten miles away, in the opposite direction—where could that rascally fellow be? Perhaps he had passed the bridge and gone lower down; but presently a man came along that road and no car had been seen, so we, having waited an hour in the rain, eventually shoulder our loads and go in search of Larry. We left him eight miles from this spot, and I will leave to my reader's imagination the horrors of that eight mile walk back. I begged a drink of milk at a cabin, half way on the road, and gave the owner of the hovel my salmon for the refreshing draught. I never was so disgusted with a fish in my life as I was with that wretched twelve pounder; he got heavier and awkwarder every mile I carried the wretched thing; and I never gave away a fish with greater pleasure! My friend sweltered along under his load, and resolutely refused to part with it; but he did suggest that now I had got rid of my fish we might carry his seventeen pounder between us, turn and turn about! My reply was not, perhaps, very courteous, but it was very emphatic, and left no room for misunderstanding as to my intentions on the subject. It still rained steadily, and it had now become very dark; the road was dreadfully rough, and was overgrown with trees, but we blundered along, keeping up a duet of abuse of that vagabond Larry. Another roadside cabin afforded us a temporary rest and shelter from the rain, and this time we get from our hospitable host a share of his supper of potatoes and buttermilk, seasoned with a sensation of the wine of the country. Here we left the seventeen pounder in exchange for the kindness and hospitality—and the good housewife was much distressed at the idea of our making any payment, even in kind. Between ten and eleven we reached the cabin where we left Larry and our car, and from the cow-shed, where the horse is stabled, comes the twinkle of a candle and the invigorating strains of a tin whistle giving the air of "Paddy Flynn's Wedding," with a high pressure gusto that stirred my companion to fury. Yes, there was Larry, on a heap of straw, with a lighted candle from the car lamp, having a musical evening all to himself, and apparently enjoying it thoroughly! "Why didn't you come down to the bridge eight miles 'beyant,' as I'd told ye, ye vagabond?" roared my host, as he seized the gossoon and shook

him as a terrier would shake a rat. Larry, between his
cuffings and shakings, managed to protest that he did not
know the way, and my friend, pausing for breath, and
holding him at arm's length, said, " What shall I do with
the scoundrel?" "Give him one for me," I replied, and
he got such another shaking up as he is not likely to forget,
and then he was flung upon the straw bellowing like a mad
bull, and invoking all the holy saints to come and save him.
We got the horse in the car and drove home, leaving Larry
to get back as best he might, and it was in the small hours
of the morning that I eventually crawled into bed. Larry
turned up next day at my place, smiling, and waylaying
me on my way to the river, asked in the most unconcerned
manner, "Did your honor and the master catch any fish
yesterday?"

There had been heavy rain for another week; the river
was again as thick as Dublin stout, and nothing less than
three or four days of fine weather would give us a chance of
a salmon. I had fired away all our cartridges in the snipe
bog, and was reduced to a state of enforced idleness that
was most trying. What could be more depressing than to
find oneself without a chum under these conditions, in a
lonely farmhouse, far from the haunts of man, and without
books? And the rain, when it really means business, rolls
along like fleecy clouds, blotting out the landscape day after
day until the trees and the rocks and everything else appear
to exude water, and there is no such thing as solid land—
the whole of the island is in a state of solution! Well, this
was the state of affairs on this occasion, and my worthy host
had tried to cheer me up by affording information as to any
mountain-fed rivers, within reach, that were likely to clear
rapidly, when the rain ceased. But of all the unreliable
guides to be met with in this world, commend me to the
Irish peasant! Host Flyn had lived, man and boy, some
sixty years, in that same farmhouse—and no keener fisherman ever cast a fly—but he knew absolutely nothing of his
surroundings beyond a range of some half-dozen miles. He
had "heard tell," however, of a good many of the angling

streams such as I was looking after. One of these, he declared, had once yielded a sackful of salmon to an English angler, when the stream was clearing, after an autumn flood. Yes, he could remember who told him—'twas Dan, the boatman. Dan was thereupon sent for, and interrogated, but he "disremembered" who told him about that sackful of salmon. The small river where they were said to have been taken ran into the big river, about ten miles lower down stream, from our house. No, he had never been up the smaller river, but he knew it was too fast and turbulent to get the boat up. Host Flyn chimed in with a lot of information that he had that morning picked up secondhand. There was a famous "carry" where the fish rested or their way up, and that was where we should get a sackful or two, at the least. By following the course of the stream upwards for about seven or eight miles, we should strike a railway, and by that means be able to get back to our own locality. There was absolutely nothing on the map to support this latter assurance, but Flyn was most emphatic, and got almost cross at my doubts. And so it was arranged that, after the rain held up for twenty-four hours, we three would explore this fabulously prolific river together. In course of time the rain ceased and away we went down stream one morning at seven o'clock, for we meant having a long day, and thus obtaining some compensation for previous enforced idleness. The big river was in rampant flood, with a froth on it like porter, and some of the low-lying land was flooded. A field of late oats, in shocks, was partly covered with water, and a big flock of ducks were in possession, enjoying themselves immensely! Both the oats and the ducks belonged to Flyn, but he thought it would be a pity to lose time in dislodging the birds—in which opinion the rest agreed, and we went past them at racing speed. Arrived at our destination, we hid the oars, padlocked the boat securely by her chain-painter to a tree, and started on our exploration. Flyn had provided a bulky lunch, including various bottles of stout, with tumblers, etc., and the whole of these things were put into the sack, which he declared to be absolutely necessary for carrying the salmon, later on. There had been a tremendous lot of water down, but the marks showed that the flood had fallen some fifteen or sixteen feet since the rain ceased. A more perfect fly-fisherman's river I never saw, alternating as it did between turbulent broken runs and deep pools; and the colour was none too high for a good sized fly, with some jungle cock in the wing. Dan and Flyn took turns with the sack and having casts with my spare salmon rod; and we tramped along, ankle-deep in the spongy, soddened land which fringed the banks. So fierce are the floods which this little river carries off that in many places the stream has cut a channel for itself from twenty to thirty feet deep, and in those lengths the going on the banks was very much better. But it was stiff work, and when we had been pegging away at it some four hours, without either seeing or touching a fish, I began to think it time we halted and repaired the wasted tissue. Dan and Flyn ate and drank their shares in ominous silence; but the latter had not given up hope—he still believed that when we reached that "carry" we should fill the sack with salmon. Thus encouraged, we started afresh; first mounting smaller flies, for the water was much shallower where we had now got to. But nothing could we move. Presently a ruined mill was discovered in the distance, and this was hailed as the vicinity of the "carry" on which all our hopes were centred. Upon getting within sight, we found four or five men stroke-hauling in the pool at the weir tail, and as many more armed with gaffs wading and waiting for any fish that attempted to run up the weir! In all, there were ten or a dozen of these poachers at work; and they went on quite unconcerned by our presence. Poor old Flyn was in despair—his last hope of a fish had deserted him! To interfere with, or even to remonstrate with, these poachers would have been sheer madness in such a lonely locality, so we sat ourselves down and watched their proceedings, packing up our rods meanwhile. That they had killed a lot of fish was quite evident, for there was a blood-stained patch on the sward where a heap of salmon had been recently lying. When our approach was signalled, no doubt these fish had been carried over to the opposite side of the river. The stroke-haulers had short rods with which they jerked a bunch of big hooks and foul-hooked their fish. We saw one killed about 10lbs., and two or three others tore out the hooks in their struggles, and escaped—to be hooked again. It was the most flagrant and barefaced piece of brutal poaching that I ever came across, and to say that I was exceedingly disgusted is not to do justice to my feelings. As the afternoon was by this time well advanced, we followed Flyn's lead and made tracks in the direction of the promised railway station. After tramping for some two hours, we reached a small cluster of cabins, where I insisted upon halting and making inquiries. "Is it a railway you want?" asked a woefully dilapidated native; and upon my replying in the affirmative, he slowly shook his shaggy head, and said, "There's no railroad in these parts!" Turning to our guide, I said, "Well, Dan, you have landed us in a fine mess! What are we to do?" His only suggestion was to go back to the boat, but to this I would not agree, as it was already getting dark, and the boat was quite fifteen miles away! If we reached her, how were we to pull her ten miles against a rampant flood? We were dog tired, and nothing in the shape of a conveyance could be got. The occupiers of the cabins gathered round us, and discussed the situation with much vehemence, in Irish, and finally my shaggy-headed friend said if we would accept such poor things as he had to offer, his cabin was at our disposal for the night. He made the offer with so much diffidence, and with such an evident desire to help us that I shook him by the hand without a moment's hesitation, and told him he was an Irish gentleman. The neighbours took him and his in for the night, and we had the cabin to ourselves. We made a hearty supper off potatoes and milk, and, with a nightcap from my well-filled flask, we then slept the sleep of the just, on a shake-down of clean oat straw. We fished back to our boat next morning, killing two salmon—12lb. and 13½lb.—on our way down, crossed the river, and got a drive home. Flyn's wife had been sitting up all night for us, and she gave him such a nagging that he suddenly remembered that the ducks were eating his oats, and rushed off to save the crop!

Of all the narrow squeaks that ever befell me in angling, about the worst was one which happened yesterday. I had been fishing our big river that was running two feet above its ordinary height, and the water was somewhat too dark for fly, except upon the shallows, where a big Jock Scot or a black and gold of the largest size sometimes scored. Truth to tell, we had for several days previously been reduced to the use of big spoons and silver Devon minnows in the bog-coloured water, and had met with but little success.

On the morning of which I am now writing I found myself some half-dozen miles down stream, below my quarters, paddling upwards a small canoe against a powerful current, and trailing a gold spoon from a short salmon-rod, in the wake of the boat. Now I am by no means an expert canoeist, and it soon became apparent to me that I had quite as much as I could do to get the crazy little craft along, without the dead pull of that long line and big spoon over the stern. Just as I was on the point of banking her, to wind up the tackle, there was a tremendous pull on the bait, and the winch flew round at a wild rate. The nose of the canoe was at once grounded, the paddle dropped, and the rod got into fighting position; but the fish had, meantime, shot across to the opposite side of the river, with a hundred yards of line out. Pressing him all that one could safely, some of the bellied line was recovered, and then it became apparent that the fish had found shelter in a leaf-covered branch, about six feet long, that had come down with the flood and got stranded. What was I to do? You cannot paddle a canoe and handle a salmon-rod at one and the same time; and after debating the "pros" and "cons" for some minutes, I decided to push off the little canoe and wind her across stream by the salmon-winch. It appeared feasible to me at the time, because the line was firmly fixed on the opposite side, and my utmost strength had failed to move the branch to which it was fast. Of course I assumed that the salmon was gone, and that the big spoon had got securely anchored. But my plan did not work out satisfactorily, for no sooner was the boat in the swift current, than she was swept down stream, the strain on the line dragged the branch afloat, and away the whole lot went towards the weir, barely two hundred yards below us! The next few seconds were about as exciting as could well be imagined: for the rod had gone overboard, and was hanging over the side, attached by a lanyard round my waist, and I was paddling frantically for the bank. The nose of the little craft grounded not twenty yards short of the dreaded weir. In less time than it takes to write this description I was on "terra firma," with the rod up, and rushing round below the fall to see what had become of that wretched branch. There was the horrid thing, bobbing about close up to the wall of the weir, at times floating out two or three yards, and then being drawn back by the under suction of that seething water. Winding in the line, every inch of which had been run off my reel, I put a steady strain on the offending bough, and eventually got it away down stream. In a shallow shelving bay the bough was stranded, and then, to my great astonishment, I discovered that the salmon was still on! He had got two turns of the treble spinning-trace round a springy branch, which had yielded to his struggles and prevented him getting a direct pull. The salmon was quite dead, and he proved to be a nice bright fish of fifteen pounds, with the sea lice on him. As I had done quite enough boating for one morning, the canoe was hauled up, I tramped home, carrying the rod and fish, and all the way it kept running through my head that something very like a fluke had saved me from losing the number of my mess.

DRY FLY-FISHING—AND OTHER THINGS

Trout fly fishermen belong to two schools—with sub-varities—the which are popularly known as up-stream dry fly-men, and down-stream "chuck-and-chance-it" anglers. I am not responsible for this classification, nor am I prepared to defend it. The dry fly fishermen, I notice, always sit in the front seats, and smile the smile of pitiful compassion upon the members of the "chuck-and-chance-it" school: Moreover, the professor of the dry fly delighteth to discourse learnedly upon ephemeræ and phryganidæ; of pseudimago and imago, and other creatures with terrible names, to the utter bewilderment of the wet fly-men ! But my present purpose is not to discuss either the scientific attainments of the one class or the hard-headed obduracy of the other. Every wet fly trout fisherman that I have come across in my travels has admitted his desire to learn the art of casting and fishing a dry fly up-stream. I verily believe that to do this successfully is the ambition of nearly every man who wields a trout rod for sport and recreation. This being so, need we feel surprised at the flutter of excitement which was caused amongst the disciples of old Isaac by the announcement that by simply painting your fly with petroleum the said fly would "float like a hay-stack." There is a vast deal more to learn in dry fly-fishing than the mere floating of your fly ; but that is the initial difficulty with the noble army of duffers; and the paraffin "discovery" was hailed by them with delight. Even some of us who claim to have passed the duffer stage thought this petroleum business would save us a lot of labour in the drying of sedges, big wickhams and other large flies, which are resorted to in those precious moments of the late evening rise. But, alas ! my experiments with flies painted, and flies soaked in paraffin, do not confirm the wonderful "discovery" as to its floating properties. I am sorry, honestly sorry, to have to condemn this bogus story of the "floating hay-stack." My experiments extended over three whole weeks' fishing, in the which I used quite fifty or sixty different flies, some soaked and others painted with the oil, and the trout shook their heads violently at these nasty flavoured morsels of fur and feather! At first I fancied that perfectly new flies floated the better for being treated with petroleum, but upon actual test, the new fly was found to keep above water quite as long as the others that were oiled. Those of us who use eyed hooks usually accumulate a goodly number of big governors, coachmen, alders, and such like flies that have lost their floating powers through the natural oil on the feathers being washed out by much use. I carefully treated a lot of these old servants to the paraffin process, and confess that my disappointment at the results was great— the flies went down like stones! So much for the promised "revolution in dry fly-fishing"—it has not come yet! If this so-called discovery had done all that its inventors claimed for it, the pupil in dry fly-fishing would still have much to learn. If some one would invent an automatic winding winch, that would keep a tight line as the floating fly comes down stream, then might the noble army of duffers rejoice, for then, and not till then, will they catch fish!

Vaseline applied to the body and hackles—but not the wings—is far superior to petroleum, but I only use it for the big absorbent bodied flies. Vaseline is far and away the best stuff to put upon your winch line in dry fly-fishing, but I am compelled to admit that it is ruinous to silk lines. I don't profess to explain the why or the wherefore, but the fact remains that I have used up four new winch lines during the three seasons that I have employed vaseline upon them. And yet I go on using it, because one dressing will last a whole day, which is more than can be said of deer's fat, or any other lubricant with which I am acquainted. Lines ought not to be greased for wet fly work, either for salmon or trout, as it fishes the flies too near the surface.

No doubt we dry fly-men are too much wedded to our system, because trout will often take a sunk fly when the river is perfectly dead, and when the superficial observer would declare that there was not a fish in the water. We all know this to be true, and yet we go on casting dry flies that the trout refuse to look at! The real explanation of this weakness—for it is a weakness—on the part of the dry fly-men is to be found in the fact that when once the art of floating a fly is acquired, down-stream fishing ceases to have any attractions. But the "chuck-and-chance-it" man occasionally has the laugh on his side, and this was the case last Saturday, when two of our professors of the "fine art" went home with empty baskets, and a "canny Scot" wiped their eye with a brace and a half of good fish!

The catching of trout with a floating artificial fly, cast up stream, is a comparatively modern art, and by common consent it is admitted to be alike the most artistic and scientific method of angling. There can be no doubt that occasionally a floating fly was used by our grandfathers, because some of the old writers speak of allowing a fly to float down stream under bushes as being a very deadly method; but this was called "shade fishing," and those old anglers who practised it would never have believed it possible to catch trout in a blazing sunshine, on a calm surface, as smooth and brilliant as a mirror. That is what the modern dry fly-men now do, using gossamer gut and microscopic flies; and I have killed many a lusty trout in the Dale that dear old Isaac Walton loved so well, under these conditions. Although my dry fly-fishing has extended over the past quarter of a century, I am by no means disposed to speak slightingly of those brothers of the craft who fish with sunk flies down stream. It is the fashion amongst some men to call them the "chuck-and-chance-it" school of anglers, but on the fast rivers of the North they would "wipe the eye" of these scoffers.

For dry fly work a short, light rod is necessary, and the lighter the rod—consistent with rigidity—the more delicate will be the casting and the greater will be the chances of sport. The best part of my own fishing is done with a ten-foot two-jointed rod, weighing seven ounces, and this is the class of weapon which finds the greatest favour amongst the most skilful exponents of the dry fly art. As to the merits of split cane over other woods for this style of fishing, there can be no two opinions, because the glued up rod can be made both exquisitely light and delicate in handling, and yet combine the spring and rigidity of a bar of finely-tempered steel. The great merit of the split cane top is its quick return, i.e., its quick response to the strike, which is of vital importance in dry fly fishing.

The tyro should seek the assistance of an old hand in selecting a rod and line suitable to his own height and strength, and to each other, and, when he has obtained these, should avoid change, except for some very great improvement. A light cane-built rod and a tapered silk line make a day's casting far less arduous than formerly.

The common fault of the costly English cane-built rods is that they are too massive and too clumsy for delicate casting and safe striking, especially where xxx drawn gut is being used. The cheap American split-cane rods err on the other side, being too "soft" (whippy) for this method of fishing. But one of my Yankee rods, that had no more backbone in it than a caterpillar, was converted into a first-class dry fly weapon by Messrs. Foster's steel wire binding process. From being a floppy, weak thing, which the fish played with when hooked, Messrs. Foster converted it into a rod with which I can now cast a long line in the teeth of a down stream wind. Several of my friends have had their rods similarly treated, and all with equally good results.

A perfectly balanced trout rod is an absolute necessity to the casting of a dry fly delicately, the slightest top-heaviness being fatal to dropping the fly as lightly as a thistle-down upon the water.

A double-tapered winch line of "medium" thickness, and a reel that will enable you to balance the rod on one finger in the middle of the cork handle are the correct things. Do not use more than four feet of gut to begin with, and let the cast commence with stout, natural gut, tapering down to the finest drawn for the two bottom links. Long casts are a mistake if you can throw a fly properly.

Various recipes are given for making the winch line float and so keeping the fly from drowning, but there is nothing that will at all compare with vaseline. Carry a little vestas box or bottle of this stuff in your pocket and anoint so much of your reel line as is used in casting. A little vaseline put upon your fly before using it will greatly increase its buoyancy, and this treatment is far superior to the use of petroleum, which some persons use and recommend to others. The "inventor" of the vaseline process was Mr. A. C. Baker, of the "Sporting and Dramatic" staff, and we fishers of the dry fly owe him a debt of gratitude for his discovery. It will rejuvenate an old fly and make it equal to new: and it is especially valuable in the case of large-winged May-flies and late evening fishing.

Having thus fully equipped the fisherman, let him turn his head up stream, and if he has choice of both banks he should choose the "weather" side, as giving him the advantage of the wind at his back in casting. Trout are always to be found waiting near the bank on the lee side of the stream for the flies that are blown over. The most successful dry fly-men all cast underhand, using only the wrist action in drying the fly, and delivering the cast with the forearm below the elbow. This delivery should be done with an upward movement, so that the fly drops of its own weight gently on the water and does not strike it with any of the force used in casting. On this method of delivery mainly depends the success of the dry fly fisherman, and I know a great many men who scare all the fish they cast for by neglecting to cultivate the knack of letting their fly fall on the water instead of throwing it there.

Another common fault amongst this noble army of duffers is the besetting sin of casting too long a line. As soon as the fly falls on the stream it begins to float down towards the man at the wheel, and the line must be shortened as it comes down, or there will be some slack between the fly and the rod top. Where such is the case you will miss every rising fish, and blame everything and everybody except yourself.

My method of shortening the line as the fly floats towards me is to gather in the slack on the thumb and little finger of my left hand, holding the rod horizontally in front of me in my right hand. By this method there is always a tight line, and the risk of missing a fish is very small indeed, if he really touches the fly. Some of those writers who profess to teach dry fly fishing, say the line should be tightened by raising the rod top, but the fly cannot be fished properly more than a few feet by that obsolete method, whereas it can be made to "fish" close up to the angler's feet by my method of using both hands. The casting of your fly lightly and the keeping of a tight line are two of the most vital points to be observed, and the third is to float your fly down stream naturally, without the slightest "drag" on the cast. If the finest gossamer gut pulls across the current it makes a tiny ripple which the trout detect. That is why so many men wade when fishing dry fly; in fact it is impossible to fish a floating fly properly in some places without wading. On a chalk stream which I haunt there is a broad, shallow pool in the village which teems with trout, but it is an utter waste of time to try for them from either of the sides. The fish are incessantly cast over by Cockney anglers, who never by any chance succeed in catching one of these trout, and yet I have seen a dry-fly man, when the duffers gave up, walk in at the tail of the pool, after hours of useless flogging, and kill a couple of brace without moving from one spot. Of course it takes a past master of the art to do that kind of thing, and it also takes a cast of xxx drawn gut and a ooo midge for the purpose. Speaking of midges, reminds me to say in this connection, that a wee Badger hackle, ooo size, with silver tag, has proved the most deadly fly in my hands that I have ever fished with. It beats all the winged black gnats that were ever tied, and, in spite of its small size, it floats splendidly when vaselined.

To become a successful dry fly fisherman it is necessary to be something of a naturalist, because the man who knows most about flies invariably kills the most fish. But there are some men who manage to get their share of trout without troubling themselves about the study of minute insect life. For myself, this study constitutes the chief charm of angling, and to master the life's history of all the teeming insects with which a trout stream abounds, is one of the most delightful studies that an angler can devote himself to. Sometimes I am disposed to think that we fishers of the floating fly are getting far too scientific and far too fastidious about fishing only with flies that are absolutely true to nature and the exact counterpart of the fly that happens to be upon the water. Of course, there are times when the fish are feeding upon some particular member of the ephemera family that they will not look at anything else, but it is doubtful whether the man who disregards nature and uses only fancy patterns would not in the long run kill as many fish as the scientific angler. This is little short of rank heresy, I know, but it is the result of my own experience, especially upon water that is very much fished.

As to the advantages of eyed hooks for floating flies, there is no room for discussion ; and although it took some time to convert me to their use, I would not use snooded hooks again if anyone would supply them free of cost. Upon the relative merits of turned up and turned down eyes for floaters there is much difference of opinion, but I am inclined to give the down turned eyes the preference, both for a straight pull and a cocked fly. In this hook you get all the weight of metal in head and barb below the water, and it acts as ballast to keep the fly upright on the surface.

Considerable importance is attached to the cocking of the fly when it alights on the water, and those who find themselves unable to acquire this knack should give up the use of winged flies and adopt hackled quills. I used them very successfully for several seasons, and found them kill even better without wings than with them. But the difficulty of getting natural hackles of the correct shades, to match the various duns, drove me back at last to the orthodox split-winged flies, except for midges.

It is much more difficult to cock a fly on the water by overhand casting than it is by the underhand process, for the reason that you throw the fly slightly upwards from the water by the latter method, and in falling it comes down by natural gravitation, wings uppermost, like a shuttlecock.

Some men adopt the rule of never casting until they find a feeding fish, but this is a great mistake, because you can often rise a trout by casting in likely places, and I never pass them over. Keep out of sight is one of the golden maxims to be observed ; and never cast your fly across the river if you can get it up stream, is another golden rule which no one can disregard and become a successful fisherman. Some exponents of the dry fly art carry this self-effacement to th extent of crawling about on their stomachs with kneecaps on, but these gymnastic performances are not. in my experience, necessary to the catching of trout, although they may be very interesting to the spectators.

Dry fly-fishing seldom kills well in the early part of the season, except upon those streams which produce a considerable amount of surface food in the months of March and April. On the chalk stream where most of my dry fly work is done, I seldom succeed in catching a basket of trout before the month of May—but there have been exceptions to this rule. Curiously enough, these exceptions have usually resulted from the use of a floating March Brown, although the river in question does not produce this fly, and the fish have not even seen the natural insect.

Upon the question of flies, I would strongly urge the beginner not to start with too many varieties. With some trepidation I recommend the following short selection : Olive Duns, dark, medium, and pale ; Ginger and Red Quill Gnats Alders, Governors, Sedges, March Browns, and Badger Hackle Midges. Every dry fly-man would be sure to declare that the list was not sufficient—that some of the best flies were omitted—but the beginner need not be afraid to meet his enemy at the river side with the above stock in his fly-box. He will be able to add to them as he gains experience, but the foregoing flies will kill trout wherever they are to be found.

In conclusion, just a few hints upon that most important subject of cutting your fly under overhanging trees and bushes. This is very easy when you know how—like a good many other things—but you must do it underhand. If there is a fish feeding close in to the bank, and he is shaded by a bush or a branch, get out the requisite length of line to cover him, swing it to and fro to get the correct aim, and when you make the forward cast, do so before the line gets fully extended behind you. The effect will be to "belly" the line, from which bow the fly will shoot forward after the "belly" has got beneath the branch. This dodge is of the utmost value to the dry fly-man, and the tyro should practise it without putting a fly on, otherwise the process of learning may prove both costly and discouraging.

GWEEDORE, CO. DONEGAL.

It is a far cry from London to Gweedore, the "ultima thule" of the wandering angler, and I undertook it with many grave misgivings. To begin with, my chum was a bad sailor, and he stipulated that we should travel via Stranraer and Larne, involving twelve mortal hours in the train from Euston station. We travelled on a Friday, and the proverbial bad luck of that day attended us from start to finish. The engine broke an axle at three o'clock in the morning, as we were approaching Carlisle, and the result was six hours' delay! When, finally, we reached Belfast on Saturday evening, the last train to Londonderry had gone, and there were no Sunday trains on the line from 'Derry to Letterkenny, which was to be our first halting place. The Belfast station-master cancelled our circular tourists' tickets, returned us our money, and sent us round by way of Dundalk to Strabane. We arrived there at dusk, and, hiring an outside car, started on a thirty mile drive to Letterkenney, where we arrived close on midnight. To say that we were worn out and weary, would not do justice to our condition—we were worse than that. Miss Haggerty was a mother to us, and her pretty little hotel furnished forth its best for our comfort and consolation, late as it was. I shall always cherish pleasant memories of this kind lady, and the solicitude which she showed towards us. Nothing more home-like and comfortable have I ever met with—and I have travelled round the whole world. Letterkenney is situated at the upper end of Lough Swilly, and there good fishing abounds in this locality ; but we had made up our minds to "do" Donegal, and my chum was deaf to all suggestions that we should break our journey and explore the angling resources of Letterkenney. And thus it happened that, after an early breakfast, we started

DONEGAL. THE POISONED GLEN.

on an outside car for that memorable drive over the highlands of Ireland to Gweedore. For rugged barrenness and utter waste of rocky desolation, I doubt if anything in the United Kingdom can be found to approach what we met with in this long drive.

Let me here explain that an "Irish mile" is in reality, about equal to a mile and a quarter by our English measurement—one of the few national institutions which have escaped the reforming hand of "Saxon" officialism! This drive of thirty Irish miles, over the Donegal mountains, takes the traveller through the wildest and most desolate portion of Ireland. There is too much of it for one day's journey, but our car-driver intimated his intention of making the return journey that same night. These Irish car horses are made to do journeys which would not be attempted by an English driver. We eased our poor beast by walking some of the steepest bits of road, and even then our horse was knocked up when we were five miles short of our destination. Lough Veagh, shown in our picture of the "Poison Glen," is a very pretty piece of trout water, but the fish it contains are only small "brownies," that are white-fleshed, and not particularly good eating. At the head of this valley stands a beautiful mansion erected by the late Mr. Adair. There is a police barracks at our end of the lake; and when we express astonishment to find such an establishment in this desolate wilderness, we are reminded of the fierce conflicts which occurred between Mr. Adair and his evicted tenants. He cleared the whole country-side of its scattered population, and the peasants ruthlessly retaliated by murdering his agents. After some very stiff climbing, we eventually emerged from a gorge where the Loughs Dunlewy and Nacung spread out before us bathed in the golden rays of the setting sun. This view was exceedingly beautiful, and, tired as we were, we loitered to note the chief points of interest in this panorama. Upon arrival at Gweedore Hotel we were calmly informed that there was no bedroom disengaged! As we had engaged our bedrooms ten days in advance, and had wired from Belfast advising the hotel people of our coming, we were considerably annoyed. But this was only the beginning of our annoyances—there were worse ones, from an angler's point of view, to follow. By dint of much pleading, we were eventually provided with a shake-down in the wash-house, an out building, where washing operations had that day been carried on. But for the strong smell of suds, and the presence of a hen with a brood of chicks, we might have grumbled less, and slept better. As it was, we spent a ghastly night, and rose unrefreshed with splitting headaches. My chum declared that he would clear out at once and go on to Carrick or the Glenties—anywhere out of this wash-house, with its suds, its chicken, and its fleas. After a frugal cup of coffee and a scrap of dry toast, he sought the manager, and requested to be furnished with our bill and also to be supplied with a car. But the manager blandly replied that our car had gone back, that there was no car kept at the hotel, and that we should have to wait until some fresh guest arrived before we could get away. What my chum said upon hearing this can be better imagined than described. I was exceedingly rejoiced to find that we were not—after this journey of 500 miles—going away without exploring the angling resources of Gweedore and its surroundings. To begin with, we made up our minds to reconnoitre the ground and decide upon our plan of action afterwards. We had seen the previous evening that there were two loughs to the south of the hotel. connected with each other by a narrow channel, and we had also noted that from these loughs flowed the Clady river. It was to fish this river for salmon and sea trout that we had journeyed these 500 miles, and when we went, on this black Monday morning, to prospect the stream, what we found will be seen in our picture of the "Salmon Ladder at Gweedore." Yes, the river was almost dried up, and the chances of getting a fish were hopeless ! And yet I had been beguiled into undertaking this journey by the statement that "The river is in good order, and there is a fair stock of salmon and sea trout." When we looked upon that salmon ladder, as depicted in our illustration, my chum gave vent to his feelings in strong language. But we really got some pretty sport

GWEEDORE: THE SALMON LEAP AT BUNBEG.

From Photo by W. Lawrence, Dublin.

after all, and, what was more, we spent a very pleasant ten days at Gweedore. Of course, salmon fishing was out of the question, and although we did waste one whole day in vain attempts to get a "fish" by trolling on the Lough, we devoted ourselves mainly to the sea trout pool at the mouth of the Clady river. This pool is tidal, but the sea trout crowd into it, waiting for a flush of fresh water to enable them to run up the river.

Should you ever journey to this "ultima thule" of the wandering fisherman, the village of Bunbeg, you will there find this ideal sea-trout pool. And, "by the same token," you are very likely to find there—at least we did—a very charming and skilful lady angler, in possession of the "rock" cast. We had been told by the courteous agent for the lessee, that the "rule of the river" was to give up a cast after fishing it fifteen minutes, if any one else claimed it. We had the "rock" cast—which was the best—and the pool being tidal it teemed with sea-trout. They literally jumped over each other's backs after the fly—a small Alexandra—and the fun was fast and furious. How long this fun had lasted is doubtful—probably more than an hour, for there were four lovely brace of sea-trout upon the sward—when we suddenly became aware that a lady angler, with her attendant, were sitting on the rocks above us, waiting for her reversion in the "rock cast." Gathering up our catch, we retired with as good a grace as could be expected of men leaving a pool full of sea-trout that rose with a bang and fought like demons. But we made our way to a cast above—in a deep gorge—and there brought up our score to ten brace, weighing 25lb. The lady at the rock pool did equally well; in fact, she beat us, in spite of our starting with four brace to the good. But she fished with a light double-handed rod, and used three flies, whilst we had been using a ten-foot 7oz. split cane, with only one fly.

The fair sex are swelling the already overcrowded ranks of fly-fishers, to the great annoyance of the "old school" of anglers, who fuss and fume at the sight of a petticoat by the riverside, and declare that "a woman's place is at home, sir." We have happily outlived this stupid nonsense. Every season adds to the ranks of lady anglers, who not only catch fish, but who show that in delicacy of casting, keenness for sport, and readiness of resource in moments of emergency, they can hold their own against their egotistical so-called "lords and masters." And those moments of emergency are by no means infrequent when the lady happens to be fishing for sea-trout, because they are amongst the gamest fish that swim, and they take nearly as much killing as a cat.

The estuaries of all the Donegal rivers frequented by these fish are swarming with them — only waiting for freshets to induce them to run up In the salt water they will take small spoons, silver Devon minnows, and the artificial sand eels, but sea-trout are very tender-mouthed creatures, and they fight so furiously, that a great many are lost when spinning is resorted to. Most of the stock flies dressed by the tackle makers for sea-trout are much too large and much too coarse for low and clear-water fishing. In fact, some of the patterns are apparently intended to frighten the fish out on to the bank. One of the best baskets of sea-trout that ever fell to our rod was killed on a dark olive dun, with quilled body, ribbed gold. If any of my angling readers have never enjoyed the splendid sport of sea-trout fishing, let them lose no time in repairing their deficiency, either in loch or river, even if they have to journey to the Hebrides in order to do so. Although these fish usually take with a rush in fast water, they often rise very gingerly in lochs, and will follow the fly some distance without touching. We had some good fun with the small brown trout, which teem in incredible numbers in both the Loughs which feed the Clady river. One evening we had an exciting bit of sport on the lower Lough. The day had been too bright and calm for sport. The sun had gone down in a blaze of fiery red, lighting up the western sky in billowy masses of golden glory. We had ceased fishing in order to watch the panoramic changes of this glorious sunset—much to the disgust of our boatman. "Isn't it a magnificent sight?" I asked him enthusiastically. "Aye,

aye," he replied, "maybe, but there's a rise away by the rushes there"—indicating a short cast on my left. More to mollify him than with any intention of trying for a fish, the fly was dropped on the spot indicated, and there came a dimple such as would be made from the rise of a three-ounce "brownie." Striking lazily, the effect was like that of a match applied to a rocket. "By jove! you're into a whacker," exclaimed my friend, as the fish tore the line off the reel, and the boatman rowed madly in pursuit. It was a grand burst, followed by a succession of skittering leaps along the surface of the water, showing us that we had a sea-trout on that would take a lot of killing. Without a wink of warning he came straight at the boat, and underneath it he went in spite of all attempts to turn him. But he reckoned without his host, for the rod was dipped around the stern and the line went clear of the keel—barring accidents his fate was now sealed. "He's a wild deil," says our boatman, as the fish makes another ugly rush and throws a somersault out of the water, and I catch a muttered malediction upon the folly of people going out "fushin' with childer's playthings." This in reference to my wee ten-foot of split cane. But the wild fury of the hooked fish was too great to last, and although the fight was a stubborn one, the little rod eventually won, and we lifted into the boat a lovely 5lb. sea-trout as bright as burnished silver. The time taken up in killing him, however, had somewhat soured our attendant, and he cut short our admiration of the fish by telling us that "there are more of them waiting to be caught if ye would only go on fushin'." Thus rebuked, we hurriedly performed those pagan rights which all true anglers observe upon such occasions, and set ourselves seriously to making the most of the last half-hour of daylight. A couple of brown trout were all that rewarded our efforts with the fly, so mounting the minnows we trolled home. My companion had the good luck to kill a 6lb. grilse within a hundred yards of our destination, and we thus went to our homely quarters well pleased with our evening's sport and at peace with all mankind.

The acompanying illustration shows a quiet corner of Lough Dunlewey, with Mount Erigal looming in the background. This is the highest mountain in Ireland, and the Donegal folk think a lot of Mount Erigal.

One of the places of interest which the visitor to Gweedore ought not to miss seeing is Skull Island. It is close to the sea-trout pool already referred to, and you can reach the island without getting wet-footed at low tide. The island is simply a mound of sand, lying off the harbour of Bunbeg; which village is three Irish miles from the Gweedore Hotel. That is a somewhat complex sentence, but the information it contains will be useful to intending visitors. And we will now get back to Skull Island and its human bones. The loose sand is here literally full of human remains, and we dug up skulls and other bones with our landing-net handles close to the surface. No one appears to know anything about the history of this singular deposit. The popular belief, amongst the natives, is that these bleached bones are the remains of the thousands who perished on this coast in the wrecked Spanish Armada.

There is excellent sea-fishing at Bunbeg, but there is great difficulty in obtaining the use of a boat for the purpose. By the way, I may mention that the cost of a boat and man on the Loughs is only five shillings per day, but the owners of the hotel are also the owners of the fishing, and they booked us a guinea apiece for salmon licenses. This we refused to pay, because we already possessed licenses. The hotel charges were reasonable—ten shillings per day—the fare was plain and plentiful, but the accommodation could not be called luxurious.

The flies with which I killed best were olive duns on Pennell's No. 1 hooks, Wickham's fancy, and Alexandras, on No. 2 hooks. For salmon, the flies used are small, and all the standard patterns will kill, provided the size is proportionate to the height of water. Of the fishing in the loughs there is not much to be said; they teem with wretched little brown trout—locally called "Jen-

GWEEDORE LOUGH.

From photo by W. Lawrence, Dublin

kins"—and you might fill a pail with these small creatures if so disposed. I did get a two-pound sea-trout in the lower lake, on small quill gnat, but that was the only exception to the small run of "Jenkins." Trolling in the upper lough is said to yield a salmon now and then, but we verified this information, and the trout taken when spinning were none over half a pound. Late autumn is about the best of the time in which to visit Donegal, but most anglers go there in the latter end of August and the early part of September. There is another very pretty lough not far from the Gweedore Hotel, where fishing can be had free for the asking; and as the trout there run to a better size, it is a place worth visiting. The name escapes my recollection at this moment.

Leaving Gweedore and going westward, the wandering angler can coast round on the mail cars and get some fishing at almost every village he comes to, with accommodation varying from fair to very good. Your journey, to begin with will take you through the Rosses to Dungloe, some fourteen miles, and there will be found a little river, with a lough at its head, and a temperance hotel, clean and comfortable. As there are sea-trout to be caught here when the river is in tune, by all means break your journey and try your luck. This little town stands on the seashore, but here, as elsewhere around the coast, the "harvest of the sea" is unreaped for the want of boat and nets.

The next village where fishing is to be got is Gweebarra, with its long tidal estuary of soft sand : but the accommodation here is shady, and a prolonged stay is not desirable. The surroundings of this quaint little village are of the wildest and most desolate character, and the total absence of vegetation adds greatly to the rugged desolation of the place. But there is a capital river, and the sea-trouting is excellent therefore the angler will not mind roughing it for the sake of sport. You must obtain permission to fish from the agent in the village.

The next halting place on the journey round the coast is Glenties, where a fairly comfortable inn will afford you all that a frugal-minded angler needs in the way of creature comforts and a clean bed. Here more trouting can be had for the asking. On leaving this little town, the country through which you pass improves somewhat in fertility, and the beautiful Glen Gesh, which leads you to your next halting place Ardara, is a glen in which you would like to linger and idle away a few hours. There is plenty of fishing at Ardara in lakes, which abound. But we must push on, for the end of this stage will land you at Carrick, and you will there find yourselves in clover, at Musgrave's hotel. There is a merry little river here, running over a rugged bed composed of huge rocks and big boulders, and the salmon leap is one of the sights of the place. But here, as elsewhere, around the Donegal coast, wet weather is absolutely necessary to sport, if you want anything better than "Jenkins." The bold seacoast about Carrick adds greatly to the attractiveness of the place and there is splendid sea-fishing in addition to the angling afforded by the river. You can put in a week here, without wanting to leave it; and when you do tear yourself away, it will be with a full determination to come again.

Killybegs is the next town in which the wandering angler halts, but the fishing in the river there is poor by comparison with some places previously visited. This portion of the drive, however, from Carrick to Killybegs, and thence on to the old town of Donegal, will delight you. It is a "famine road"—made to give relief to the distressed in the bad times—and it runs through lovely coast scenery, skirting the shore.

As for old Donegal town, there is little beyond its antiquity to commend it to the angler's favour. But there is a river passing through the town itself, and forming the only outlet for the waters of Lough Eask. There are some disputes about the rights of fishing both upon lough and river at this place, but the Saxon visitor will be cordially welcomed, and need not trouble himself about the local squabbles. The fishing here is best in the late summer, as sea-trout are then plentiful, and their presence compensates for all other shortcomings. At Donegal town you again strike the railway—at least there is a station three miles out of the town—the money failed at that stage!

A word of advice in conclusion; burden yourself with as little luggage as possible, carry only one rod, avoid talking politics and as you value your peace of mind, never look into an Irish kitchen!

The way to see Ireland properly is to discard railway travelling, and to drive through the country on an outside car, stopping whenever objects of interest are found, and holding converse with the people at every opportunity.

If you expect to beguile the tedium of your journey by listening to the tales and jokes of your car-driver, you will be grievously disappointed, because the witty Irish coachman exists only in books. It is true that a drunken rascal, who drove me one of the stages round Donegal, said a smart thing. Going down a hill as steep as the side of a house, this reckless Jehu urged his horse into a gallop. Holding on like grim death, I expostulated in vain.

"Mike, you villain," said I, "what do you think would become of me if the horse went down?"

He laughed, as he replied. "'Twould depend on your past life, your honour!"

In this way, I have just completed a journey of a hundred and seventy miles, going round the whole of the north-west coast; and I am leaving it full of sorrow for the condition of the poor people who inhabit it, and struggle against the forces of nature in their vain effort to extract from this rocky, barren soil the means wherewith to eke out a miserable existence. The whole of this district which I have traversed during the past few weeks is treeless, and the soil, if it can be termed soil, is peat, wet, cold, and boggy, but there is very little of this poor stuff available for cultivation, because of the huge rocks which bestrew the ground and underlie its surface. Some of these poor tenants of plots not more than three or four acres in extent said they had paid no rent for several years, and were quite unable to do so by reason of bad seasons and bad prices. What the seasons are like here may be imagined when I say that the hay harvest has only just begun, in the first week of September, and many of the oat patches are still as green as grass. With regard to prices, they are ruinous to the producer, yearling calves realising but 30s., whilst mutton was being retailed at 4d. per pound wherever I inquired its price. Geese were a drug in the market at 1s. to 1s. 6d. each, chicken from 5d. to 7d. apiece, and butter 5d. per pound. If it be thought that these low prices are favourable to cheap living on the part of the Irish tenants, let me correct such a grave mistake, for none of these luxuries are consumed by the producer. His diet consists of Indian meal, potatoes, and seaweed, the few poor animals he is able to rear being the only saleable commodities upon which he relies to bring him in a bit of money. Pigs are very scarce throughout the north-west coast of Ireland; in fact, you will not meet half a dozen in a day's drive, the explanation being that there is not sufficient food to keep them. Sheep take the place of "Dennis," and nearly every cottar has one or two little mountain sheep, no bigger that small English lambs, and the selling value of these animals varies from 10s. to 12s. apiece. Passing through the Rosses, over the moor, from Dungloe to Glenties, I came across vast numbers of the insect-eating plant—the sundew—made famous by Darwin; and I may also mention that here, too, the Osmundi fern grows luxuriantly, huge belts, fully four feet in height, being frequently met with. No one can visit this part of the Emerald Isle without feeling curious as to the alleged manufacture of "potheen," as the spirit distilled by illicit means is called. Several important functionaries assured me that the trade had been suppressed, fines of £50 and the alternative of twelve months in prison having stamped out this smuggling trade. I had my doubts upon this subject from the first, and now those doubts are confirmed, for in the fastness of a mountain top, I saw unearthed a store of the "cratur," and, what is more, I tasted of the forbidden cup. It was colourless, and in flavour strongly resembled Hollands gin, whilst its strength was sufficient to blow the roof of your head off! Let me here record the fact that throughout the whole of my journeying I have met only one man the worse for drink, and that was at Mountcharles market. That illicit distillation exercises demoralising influences upon the people wherever it is carried on cannot for a moment be doubted, and not the least serious injury it entails is the loss of grain used for the purpose, to say nothing of the laziness, lawlessness, and misery which it brings in its train. The priests and the police do all they can to suppress this pernicious trade, but the character of the country favours the manufacture of "potheen"; for here you find nature in her wildest moods triumphant, and man nowhere—for rugged mountains, vast loughs, deep gorges, bogs, and wild desolation, this coast of Ireland is unparalleled. But I came here on a fishing trip, and ought not, perhaps, to have gone scouring about the country on cars. poking my nose into all the affairs of the natives, hob-nobbing on mountain tops with ragged and grimy rascals who defraud Her Majesty's revenue; but the truth is that this paradise of the angler stands greatly in need of a fortnight's rain, and without it the salmon will not rise to a fly. Sea-trout are to be had in abundance, but they are a poor substitute for the king of fish, and so it happens that I have packed my rods and gone wandering over the country, learning all I can of the condition of its people.

AUTUMN NORFOLK TROUTING.

The land of the Broads is the paradise of the bottom fisherman, and there are very few south of England anglers aware of the fact that several excellent trout streams exist in the Eastern counties. I recently spent a few days on the "Wensum," and there had capital sport, in spite of the weather being both wet and boisterous. "Wensum? Where on earth is the Wensum?—never heard of it before!" These will no doubt be remarks which the foregoing sentence will provoke amongst those slayers of trout who are ever on the look-out for fresh fields and pastures new. Whether or not any of this water is open to the public, I am not in a position to state, but the length of river fished by myself and friend is very strictly preserved, and it has had a considerable amount of money and labour expended upon re-stocking it with trout. We left the train at the nearest point, and a drive of some eight or ten miles landed us at a quaint little village, with a straggling old inn, capable of housing the scanty population of the whole parish. A friendly "agent in advance" had secured us quarters in this quiet hostelry, but its internal appearance was not luxurious—sanded floors, spotless deal tables, and well-scrubbed wooden forms, being the barrack-like furniture of the "sitting-room" into which we were ushered. But those of us who have fished all over the world, out of sheer love of the sport, make light of domestic discomforts where fish are to be caught, and so we entered into our new quarters with all the cheerfulness of a Mark Tapley. We penetrated to our bedrooms, up creaky old stairs, and along a corridor, both bare of carpet, and redolent of apples, onions, and pumpkins, which it appears to be the custom of this country to store in the upper chambers. A short truckle bed is not an ideal couch for a man of 5 ft. 10 in., but it can be lengthened with a chair; and it is good for us to mortify the flesh occasionally, if only that we may the better appreciate our own homes! I am not going to inflict any more of these domestic details upon you, except that I shall touch with a flying finger upon the savoury repast of pigs' fry which our hostess set before us, and leave you to imagine how we two miserable dyspeptic wretches collapsed at the sight of this solitary dish! But we were on fishing bent, and not to be discouraged by trifles. Had we not fished together, year after year, through all the wildest and most "dissolute" parts of Ireland, and there been content with salmon steak or toasted trout, potatoes and buttermilk, and a shake-down of oat-straw at night? And now let me introduce you to the river, which we approach through a richly wooded park, heavily stocked with both fur and feather, and here we commence operations in a lovely pool, some thirty yards wide, and a hundred yards long. The Wensum is a slow running stream, about equal in size and volume to the Itchen, above Winchester; but this Norfolk stream is slower, and has a soft bottom which makes wading impossible. Waders, however, are necessary to your comfort, if the weather is at all wet, because the banks are very bad in places. The river consists of long sections of shallow, smooth-surfaced, slow water, little more than a foot or two in depth, alternating with deep reaches, containing big holes, which afford shelter to the pike. These rapacious pests have hitherto defied all the persistent efforts made to exterminate them; in fact, they appear to thrive upon the persecution to which they are subjected. Looking over the road-bridge, at the tail of the pool, where we decided to commence, we saw such a shoal of aldermanic roach, which our attendant called "red fins," as I had never seen before. There were hundreds of them, in about 8 ft. of water, and they were all specimen fish, from a pound upwards! I am not a float fisherman, but the sight of these fat fellows made us wish that we were armed with the proper weapons to tempt them to destruction.

There was a gusty half gale blowing in our teeth, and

my little 7 oz. ten-foot rod did not enable me to fish the broad shallow properly, but the shallow contained a goodly number of rising trout, who were taking a pale, watery, olive dun, and I stuck to this hundred yards of water nearly the whole day. It had not been cast over for several months, and the fish were not at all gut shy, but they were feeding fully twenty yards from my bank, under the shadow of some big timber trees that made fishing from the opposite side impossible. It was hard work, and the oozy nature of the soil prevented wading—you sank to your knees in a tenacious quagmire that held you fast! My score was only three brace, but they weighed 8lbs.; and he would be a greedy fisherman who was not content with such a basket. The other fisherman had not fared so well, but he had turned his back to the wind and gone down stream with the keeper, who initiated him into the art of floating a worm before him, close in to the bank. A brace of trout, 3 lbs., were thus ignominiously killed; and we went home to find ready for us another meal from the domestic pig! Next day it blew great guns down stream, and rained in torrents, and dry-fly fishing was therefore an utter impossibility. We sheltered ourselves as best we could behind the stems of some big trees that overhung a deep pool, and there wasted the forenoon until, having disposed of lunch, our attendant keeper suddenly remembered that the squire had a lot of minnows stored in a tank! Away went "Velveteens," and presently returned with a stable pail containing a lively lot of bait, and we had, meanwhile, stripped some old May flies of their dressings, and mounted natural trout gut casts. The keeper produced a cartridge, loaded with No. 5 shot, which we split, and then we were ready for the fray. I tried a cast in the pool beneath the tree where we had stood all day; got a run first time and struck, with the result that the line came back minus minnow and hook! Then I mounted another bait, and repeated the performance, with exactly the same results! My friend, a few yards below me, had been more successful, for he was fast in a pike of four or five pounds, and the fish did just as he pleased. Away he went tearing down stream, the little trout rod being perfectly powerless to control the brute. For nearly half an hour this unequal fight went on, the little ten foot of hickory being bent like a hoop, for its owner is a very unskilful fisherman; and finally the rod smashed off short at the swell of the butt, and the pike broke away! Fortunately we had a spare rod with us. Going back to my old post, I put another minnow over the same spot, and was taken immediately, but by striking the moment the line checked, the fish was safely hooked this time, and a pretty fight we had.

As an illustration of what seven ounces of split cane will do, if those who handle it keep cool, this struggle afforded a very striking example. It was unfair, perhaps, to put one's pet dry-fly rod to such a task; but we were in for it now, and the suggestion of my friend, "Cut your line and let the brute go," fell upon deaf ears. There was plenty of water, and no weed-bed within fifty yards below us, so that, barring accidents, I had no fear of the results. The pike contented himself at first with moving around his old quarters in a small circle, and treating the slight resisting power of the rod with contempt; but presently he got alarmed, resented the strain, and made two or three ugly rushes, coming back each time to the same old spot, about a dozen yards from the bank, in eight or nine feet of water. By and bye he became very uneasy, shook his head savagely, and the nervous tremor of his body came up to the rod-butt like a telephonic message. Look out for squalls— he was going to show fight! The question of what he would do did not long remain in doubt; with a wild rush he tore up stream into the shallows above, where, leaving a wake behind him like a barge, he ploughed along with his tail and back fin out of water. For fully a hundred yards he went, and we both raced after him as hard as we could go, but no haven of shelter or friendly weed-bed could he find. Then he halted, and we got on level terms with him once more; but catching sight of us on the bank, back he went like an express train to his old quarters. Twice were these tactics repeated, and then, pumped out and exhausted, he rolled over close to the bank, and Velveteens cleverly tailed him, and flung him out on the bank, a well-fed fish of 6lbs., with my lost tackle still in his mouth.

It continued to rain, and the gale still raged, and we therefore gave up for the day, to return to a dinner of more pork! This pig diet was getting serious, so we had some pike steaks fried, but as these were cooked in pork fat, the flavour of the unclean animal was very much in evidence. Talk of pigs being the domestic pets of the Irish people, why I verily believe that "Dennis" is the only edible creature known to the rural population of the eastern counties.

Next day the prospects were better, the gale had expended itself and the sun shone, so we were early at the riverside. By way of a beginning we got chased by an able-bodied shorthorn bull, and if he had not considerately given us two hundred yards start, we might not have done any fishing at all that day. I never covered the ground and got over a gate quicker in my life, and the language that beast used towards us from the other side must have been awful, if we had only been able to understand him! As he appeared disposed to charge the gate, we did not stop to discuss the matter with him. What is the proper course for an angler to adopt when he is charged by a bull? This is a question fraught with most vital importance to us all, because most anglers meet with these bovine incidents now and then—this makes my fourth encounter in five years! The only man who ever answered my question, told me that the best thing to do was to seize the bull by his tail, and belabour him with gaff or landing-net handle. This may be a good plan, but none of the bulls that have chased me ever came tail first!

We fished at different lengths of the river to-day, and found the trout close up to the bank, and mostly hid beneath the shade of overhanging tufts of grass, or other shelter, so that to float a fly over them was, in most cases, impossible. Velveteens had no faith in the fly for these bank feeders, and I dare say he was right from his point of view, but we were fishing for sport, and not for the pot, and therefore I would have none of his worms. My companion in arms, however, yielded to his solicitations, and away they went together, to some famous hatch-hole that the keeper knew of. At lunch time they turned up again, with a lovely 3lb. trout that had been wormed out of his stronghold. The impression conveyed to my mind by these Wensum trout was, that they were harried incessantly by the pike, and, as a consequence, were always hiding themselves in shy places and amongst weeds in shallow water. Four brace rewarded my efforts—the red quill gnat proving the best fly—and the best fish weighed $1\frac{3}{4}$lbs., the rest averaging a pound each. I neither saw, nor did I catch, any small trout, and it is my belief that there are quite as many jack as there are trout in this river. But no matter, it runs through rich meadows, and you fish amidst pleasant surroundings, and, given more comfortable quarters wherein to roost, with some variation of the swinish diet, I hope next season to renew my acquaintance with the Norfolk trout.

THE BANN AT COLERAINE.

The accompanying illustrations will afford the reader a very good idea of the magnitude of this splendid river weir the river is tidal, and salt water, at spring tides, forces its way up to the town, which is half a mile below the "cuts." These are salmon traps, which occupy the centre portion of the weir, a "queen's gap" being the only space left through which ascending fish can escape the trappers. Below the weir, the fishing is free, but above this barrier the Bann Club charge a guinea per week for the right to fish. The weir-pool and race are often crowded with fresh-run fish, and it is a good fly water, the best flies being the Dunkeld, Judge, and Silver Doctor. A narrow platform extends across the top of the weir, and the lessees of the "cuts" use this platform to enable them to net out the salmon which are captured in the traps. The number of fish thus taken is enormous, as may be inferred from the fact that the lessees pay an annual rent of £5,000 for their rights. These traps are really square cages of lattice-work, into which the ascending salmon are able to enter, from whence they cannot escape. Upon the occasion of our inspecting these "cuts," my companion was fired with a desire to become the possessor of a grand twenty-pounder which entered one of the traps whilst we were looking on. It was my chum's first salmon-fishing experience, and he had yet to catch his first fish. But the idea of sending home that splendid salmon, and allow the wife of his bosom to suppose he had caught it, took possession of his mind, and do it he would. Giving his card and a sovereign to the man in charge of the "cuts," my friend directed the fish to be sent to his address in Kent. My friend wrote, announcing to his wife the cap-

THE BANN AT COLERAINE.

From photo. by W. Lawrence, Dublin.

ture of a magnificent salmon and telling her it was on its way to her home. The clever little woman wrote an ecstatic letter, eulogising the beauty of the fish and the prowess of her lord and master. And he fairly beamed with delight over this successful piece of deception; but Nemesis is sure, though slow of foot. That man at the "cuts" not only forwarded the fish, but he subsequently sent a note, explaining that he found that the salmon did not weigh quite so much as they supposed, and he therefore enclosed 2s. 6d. in stamps, as change out of the sovereign! The wife kept this communication to herself until fully a week after her husband's return, and until he had involved himself in a labyrinth of falsehood as to the full details of how he caught that first salmon. Then she gave him the letter and the stamps, and then he wanted to go straight off to the "cuts," at Coleraine, and pitch that wretched man over the weir, into the whirlpool below! But, in justice to my chum, I must say that what he told his wife about the catching of that fish was what happened when he really caught his first salmon. Only he did not tell her that it was only a poor little eight-pounder, nor did he say that he trembled so much with excitement that he could scarcely hold his rod and begged me to take it from his hands. He also omitted to mention that he went down on his knees before his prize as it laid upon the bank and stroked it lovingly, declaring it to be the very finest salmon he ever saw in his life! A woman's first baby is not to be compared with a man's first salmon.

The free water between the weir and the town of Coleraine holds some very fine trout, but they are not much fished for, and, considering the size of the town, I was astonished at the absence of local anglers. We put up at the Clothworkers' Arms during our stay, and were influenced in doing so by the fact that some members of the Royal Irish Society were stopping at this house. I relied upon the sound judgment of these London Aldermen, and was not disappointed. This committee of the London Corporation come over once a year to inspect their possessions, and to hear applications or representations from their tenants.

I may here conveniently explain that the River Bann, from the sea to the lough from whence it flows, is the property of the London Corporation. They lease the whole of the fishing rights to a limited liability company, of whom Mr. Moore is the managing director, the rent paid by the company amounting to £5,000 per annum. The company carry on all the salmon netting and trapping themselves, but they have sublet the rod-fishing from Coleraine "cuts" to Portna Weir—about twenty miles— to the Bann Angling Club. These gentlemen reserve the best portion for the use of their own members, and issue weekly tickets at a guinea per week to strangers. Trout-fishing, from the bank, is free to all-comers; and I know of no river in Ireland which produces such trout as the Bann, either for quantity, size, or quality. It is a slow river, except in the vicinity of the weir, and a dry-fly trout fisherman will find it an ideal stream for the exercise of his scientific method of fishing.. Pale Olive Duns, Claret Spinners, Brown Sedges, of varying shades, Iron Blue Duns, Wickhams, and Black Gnats are amongst the best flies to be used as floaters.

THE BANN ABOVE COLERAINE WEIR.

From photo by W. Lawrence, Dublin.

THE BANN AT KILREA.

AUTUMN ANGLING.

Paraphrasing a well-worn adage let me preface my remarks upon autumn fishing by saying that none of it is bad, only some forms of it are better than others. Personally, I have a predilection for the catching of freshly-run, autumn salmon, and I am prepared to join issue with all and sundry who speak contemptuously of this branch of our sport. It is not the capture of "potted" fish—as red as a copper coal-scuttle—that delights me; it is those big, heavy fellows that I go for, who defer their return to fresh water until the autumn floods give them a clear course to their breeding grounds. There are not a great many Irish rivers which get this late run of clean fish, but I know a few that do, and on these it has been my habit, for many years past, to wind up the back end of the fly-fishing season. With your gun to fall back on, when the river is running as thick as Dublin stout, there are snipe to be had for the asking in this hospitable island, wherever a bog exists—and where is the watershed that does not abound in bogs, and "snipes"? Sea trout there are, too, in plenty; if you only go to the right places; but with the approach of October, I am satiated with the slaughter of "trouts," I want something more substantial. With that craving for "fresh fields and pastures new," which is common to our craft, I have wandered from one river to another, in pursuit of autumn sport, but I always drift back to my old love, the Bann, and confess, with something akin to shame, that in running after something better, I have—like the dog in the fable—grasped at the shadow and lost the substance. Taken all round, the Bann, from the middle of September to the end of October, is one of the best rivers in Ireland for autumn salmon fishing. This river has a distinct run of late fish, heavy fellows, clean and full of fight. But rod fishing now closes at the end of September.

This Kilrea section of the river is the favourite location of those anglers who fish the "guinea water," and as I have only missed visiting it one season, out of the past sixteen years, I ought to know something about it. But first let me say, for the information of English anglers, that the very when it reaches the last weir, at Coleraine. Below this best route to the Bann is via Liverpool to Belfast, and thence by Northern Counties line. If you want to go to Coleraine, this is the direct route, and if you decide upon going to Kilrea, book to Cullabackey from Belfast. The mail car will take you to Kilrea for half-a-crown, or you can charter a private car to carry you the ten-mile drive for five shillings. After a long journey, by rail and sea, this drive on an "outside" car—taking care to sit on the left side—is most enjoyable. As you leave Cullabackey pull up on the bridge, and have a look at the course of the River Maine. It is an exceedingly pretty stream from this point up to Carryford, running through a richly wooded valley, and it holds some splendid trout, the fishing being free. Later in the autumn the salmon come up from Lough Neagh, and I have had fair sport in the Maine after rain, when the Bann was too high and too thick to fish.

The scenery on the road to Kilrea will gratify both the eye and mind of an angler escaped from the toil and moil of City life, and the panorama of moor and mountain will amply compensate him for adopting this route instead of travelling to Kilrea by rail. Yes, you can do it by rail from Belfast, if you possess your soul with sufficient patience, and can find any recreation either of mind or body in a weary railway journey. But you will save nothing—or next to nothing—in money by wasting half a day in doing a train journey, which can be done in half the time by the Cullabackey road route. As regards quarters at Kilrea, to those who take their ease at their inn, there is the Mercers' Arms, newly rebuilt, where

Host Kirk will treat them well, and make them comfortable. I have always found a warm welcome with frugal farmhouse fare, and lovely beds to sleep on, at the foot of Kilrea Bridge. My old friends, John Blair and his wife, are there the ideal host and hostess of a wandering angler, who is content with such good things as a farm produces. The river is within a stone's throw of their house, and this is no small consideration to a man who is keen on sport, and who does not want to waste his time and strength by tramping to and from his quarters. John is a dear lover of fishing, and a goodly portion of his life has been spent beneath the shade of a beloved "sally-bush," with a big bunch of worms on, waiting for one of those "bully trouts" to gorge the tempting morsel. And there are such "trouts" in close proximity to Kilrea Bridge, and John's "sally-bush," as would fire the imagination of any angler. Looking over the parapet of Kilrea Bridge—down stream —I have seen a score of big trout, ranging from a pound to four pounds apiece, sucking in Duns, from the surface, with a steady persistence that showed they were in earnest. The difficulty is to approach them in a boat, without putting them down, and when you hook one look out for squalls. I have seen them take fifty or sixty yards of line off the reel at one dash, and fight with all the stubborn resistance and sustained energy of a salmon. In fact, I played one of these three-pound trout on a light salmon rod and was so fully convinced I had a "fish on" that we went to the bank to gaff him. Although some of the Bann trouting can be done from the bank, a boat is really necessary to enable you to command the best fishing. And you cannot use a boat unless you possess a guinea ticket for salmon fishing.

These guinea tickets confer the right to fish for salmon and trout from a boat between Portna Weir and Movanagher Weir, a distance of about four miles, or it may be a little more. As the river is navigable, and the water is held back by these weirs, it follows that the stream is too slow for effective salmon-fly casting, but there are a few fly casts which invariably hold fish. Commencing at the upper extremity of the guinea water, at Portna Weir, our illustration of McCarroll, the lock keeper, gaffing a salmon, gives us the first bit of "fly water." The break shown in the weir is a salmon ladder, and running fish that are waiting to ascend it hang about in the easy water below on this side of the river; the force of the stream being greater in the centre and on the opposite shore. With a fairly good height of water, this quiet corner is always a safe find for a salmon; and the next bit of fly-water is from the "pier" down to the "Camlet," along the left bank of the river. There is a shallow bit along the eastern shore, after passing the "Camlet," which always holds fish in high water, and then you go through the arches of the bridge. From the post, in the river, opposite John Blair's "sally-bush," will pay for fishing carefully with a fly, as there is a ridge which runs across the river's bed at this point, and the salmon rest behind it. This is locally called a "stank," which, being interpreted, means a wall. The Bann abounds in "stanks," and whenever you come across one you may count with certainty upon finding a fish there ready to take a fly—that is, if there are fish going. Captain Armstrong's cast is a good bit of fly-water, but there is not enough stream to make it duffers' work, and you must be able to manipulate a fly pretty fairly in order to score at this point. This is one of the first places on the guinea water which fish a fly after a flood, and a big Jock Scott will often yield a fish here before the porter tint has gone out of the water. The same remarks are true of the shallows beneath the wood, at Moor's Lodge, which is situate nearly at the lower end of our guinea water. It will be gathered from the foregoing that the Bann is not a first-class fly-fishing river for salmon, but to that noble army of duffers who do not disdain to troll a minnow or spoon, or even to "harle" his salmon flies, this river is an ideal amateur angler's paradise! Without quite ranking myself as a duffer, I have found the Bann fishing good enough to tempt me, over a long period of years, and I hope yet to pay many more visits to the "Bann shore."

PORTNA WEIR, KILREA.

Photo from G. Dallas, Coleraine.

The glorious uncertainty of salmon fishing is proverbial, and therein lies one of its chief charms With water very low and stale, a scalding sun, and an east wind, we commenced operations last Saturday, and nothing could have been more depressing than our prospects of sport. Said an old croaker, who shares our farmhouse quarters, " I have been here a month, and only caught four salmon." We told him it was due to his not being able to fish; for hope springs eternal in the breast of the fisherman, and he always believes himself able to succeed where others have failed. At any rate, we started with an eleven pounder that afternoon, by way of beginning, and on Sunday the wind veered to the south and worked itself up to half a gale. This lasted through the night, and although the rain held off, there was no sun on Monday, and the river was lashed into life by a rattling breeze. There were "lashins o' fish" in the water, and my chum was up and at them by six o'clock. I have long since come to the conclusion that early rising is a mistake, and when I came down at 8.30 and saw the pretty eight pounder that had rewarded the early riser I was not in the least envious—he had earned the prize. We started together at ten o'clock, and he scored a seven pounder within one hundred yards of the house. Then I was envious, but congratulated him on his luck notwithstanding. You can forgive your friend anything else but you cannot forgive him catching more fish than you do. About a hundred yards lower down I had my revenge by hooking a very sporting fish, but my pleasure was short-lived, for after playing her for about five minutes she made a flying leap, and dropping the point of rod, in orthodox fashion, the fly fell out of her mouth! She was a clean, fresh run fish of about twelve pounds, and I felt bad, very bad, for the next quarter of an hour. The English language is too poor to enable an angler to do justice to his feelings under such conditions.

I told my boatman, Cornelius O'Hara, that if he did not put me into a sixteen or seventeen pounder before lunchtime he would be dismissed without a character. He replied quite seriously, "Very well, your honour, I'll do it. Shall we go up or down stream?" I remarked that it was for him to find the fish, and therefore left him to make his own choice. "Put on a silver minnow" said he. "We will go up to the pier." This is a tongue of land just below the tail of the Portna Weir, shown in illustrations. We mounted the minnow on a fine trace of annealed steel wire, no thicker than a piece of trout gut, with only one swivel in the head of the Devon and another at the end of the winch line. For fishing in low, clear waters this wire is invaluable, and of the many scores of salmon and pike that I have killed upon it, I never had an accident with it, or lost a fish through breakage. As we started the boat, I threw my minnow some distance astern, and jumped it up and down in the water to get out line. Whilst doing so there was a tremendous pull, which nearly snatched the loosely-held rod out of my hands. "A fish!" I exclaimed, and pushing the boat to the shore, we fought it out on the bank, but the fish gave a flying leap, and we saw at once that it was a big trout, and not a salmon, that we had on. He fought gamely, but ultimately came to net, and he had blown the silver minnow up the nine foot steel trace over the top swivel, and it was there suspended when the net was put under the trout. I give this experience of a fish blowing the bait out of its mouth because there is a conflict of opinion amongst our fishing authorities upon this subject. Personally, I have no doubt whatever as to the powers of propulsion possessed by trout and salmon, in expelling either a fly, worm, or minnow. Not that I ever caught a trout or a salmon on a worm in my life, but I have seen them so caught, and I have also seen a bunch of worms blown several feet up the trace, over coarse knots in thick salmon gut. But this is a digression, for which, perhaps, I ought to apologise, and get back to that big trout, which we have left all this time on the grass, close to old John Blair's "sally-bush." The old soldier, who haunts this particular spot in quest of "trouts," looks at our three-and-a-half pounder, and opines that it is a beauty. Old John foregathers, and patronisingly remarks, "It's not a bad trout, but it's only a baby compared to some of them hereabouts." We send it to the farmhouse, close by, to be cooked for our dinners, and re-enter the boat. "Now, Cornelias," I say, "we must have that sixteen or seventeen pounder, or else you will be out of employment this afternoon." He smiles one of his knowing smiles, and as he settles to his oars, suggests, "Maybe we'll find what you want at the Camlet." Away we went with the silver minnows over the stern, and at one of the least likely spots in this length of the river a fish took my lure, with a gentle "tug," deep down. He showed little fight at first, and I said "He is only a little one;" but upon giving him the "butt" it became evident that he was a big fish. Going off with a rush he fought stubbornly in nine foot of water, and all efforts to raise him nearer the surface were unavailing for a long time, in spite of a powerful rod strained almost to breaking point. Finally we got him to close quarters, but show himself he would not until he rolled up to the surface and was cleverly gaffed by our attendant, "Cornelias." A grand male fish he proved to be, weighing sixteen-and-a-half pounds, in excellent condition; and if those persons who say that autumn fish will not fight ever have the good luck to get hold of one like him, their arms and back will ache before they finish him off. Going back to the bridge, where my chum had killed his two fish, I got into a very pretty little seven pounder, which was safely grassed, and after this nothing more could be done, except that my chum killed a pike on a minnow. It was not a brilliant day's sport, perhaps, but it was good enough to satisfy yours truly, and it made that old croaker green with envy! Our score for the day had beaten his record for a month in weight. Perhaps some of my angling readers will also feel a little envious of our good luck, but I can only say if they do, "Come over to Ireland and share it."

Since the foregoing was written I have been getting some very good sport amongst the Bann salmon, our score for the week being thirteen fish, weighing 113lb. This is not a big average, but, with one exception, they were all bright, fresh run fish, in splendid condition. The rain still holds off, and six weeks have now elapsed since a drop of water fell on this thirsty soil. As the spring of the year was very wet, the potato crop was late in planting, and the drought of the past few weeks has, therefore, been very beneficial in ripening what few tubers have escaped disease. These are very few, however, and the crop will not be more than one-third of an average yield. Oats are an enormous crop—the best that has been known for many years—and the same may be said of flax, judging from the number of stinking flax pits with which the whole of the N.N.W counties now reek. By reason of the drought there is little, if any, of this vile-smelling flax water in the rivers, and the salmon, as a consequence, rise well and give good sport to the angler. On the river that I am fishing, the run of salmon this season, from the sea, has been the largest within the memory of the oldest fishermen. The river swarms with fish, and we only want a freshet to raise the water about a foot, and then our score for last week could be doubled without any difficulty. The two best fish taken on our beat last week were $19\frac{1}{2}$lb. and $21\frac{1}{2}$lb., but neither of these fell to my rod. $16\frac{1}{2}$lb. was my best. Our thirteen salmon in one week beat the record for any boat on the river this season; but we also had a turn amongst the pike, killing about twenty, besides several big trout.

Following on the storms which last week made fishing impossible in Ireland, we have had such alternations of sunshine and cloud, and such balmy breezes, as seldom fall to the lot of an autumn salmon angler. The floods of last week have brought up those laggard fish, who hang about the estuary of this big river, until the heavy rains of October, or November, give them a free run up to their breeding grounds. But before going further, let me explain that I am located in a farm house in the County of Antrim upon the banks of the river Bann—a river quite as large as the Thames. The Bann is the only outlet of the waters of lough Neagh—a mighty inland sea, some thirty miles long by nine miles wide. As lough Neagh receives the water of half-a-dozen different rivers, and only has one outlet (the Bann) you will understand that my present fishing ground deserves to rank amongst the chief rivers of the United Kingdom. This being so, it carries, as befits its importance, big fish, and many of these big fellows put off their annual visits to fresh water until the floods enable them to get over the weirs without difficulty. Having thus cleared the ground, let me proceed to tell you that last week's raging flood brought up the autumn run of fish, and it only remained for us anglers to possess our souls with patience until the water settled down into fishing order. How anxiously we watched the gradual changes from the consistency of double stout to that of single porter; and how regularly we consulted the water-gauges to note the gradual decrease in the flood. On Monday the local oracles declared that "she" was fishable—that there was just a chance. Why rivers are always spoken of as belonging to the feminine gender by fishermen has always puzzled me, and the only explanation which suggests itself to my mind, is that trivial causes serve to upset rivers, and that gentle treatment is the only method to woo them back to smiles and dimples. Well, well, I am at a safe distance from home, and that paragraph can therefore stand. As I mentioned just now, Monday was said to afford a chance, and although there was a decided tinge of porter in the stream, my boy Mike said he had known "Three big bastes" killed in an hour, at a certain spot, close handy, under precisely similar conditions to these. But the worst of Mike is, that he always does remember something which he believes will please you. Thus, on our way to the boat, I pick out what I think is a likely fly to kill on such a day as this, and Mike at once declares that he now "dis-rememers" that this was the very pattern on which the aforesaid three fish were killed in the "dirthy watter." It is unnecessary, perhaps, to add that we never moved a fish at the cast relied upon by Mike; but it is only fair to him to say that as we were tramping home tired, dispirited and dejected, late in the afternoon, he clutched me by the sleeve and exclaimed: "Blessed Saints; did you sa the baste?" I had not seen the "baste," and to tell the truth, I did not believe that Mike had seen a salmon rise; but yielding to his vehement protestations, I fished over the spot and at the second cast up came a nice little fish of about ten pounds, and we bagged him. On Tuesday the river was still too high, both as to volume and colour, and Mike went bog trotting with me in the forenoon, and retrieved five or six brace of snipe out of bog holes, often up to his waist in water—in the absence of a dog. Later on, we had another go for a salmon, when a glorious old Bann trout, of four pounds' weight, took the salmon fly, and after a stubborn fight, was gaffed by Mike; who, whilst giving him the "coup de grace" by wacking his skull with a boulder, called him all the "owld bastes" and "ugly devils" that he could think of. On Wednesday we poled a cot over the foaming waters of the weir tail, and had some good sport under the falls. First a wretched pike, of six or seven pounds, came up with a "boil," like a salmon, and when struck, he bolted down stream, necessitating our following, in order to save the casting line. The hard labour of an hour was thus wasted, and the fresh water shark, when killed, proved to have mangled a new "Black ranger" into a shapeless mass of fur and feathers. How the boatmen anathematized him, and how Mike kicked him savagely at intervals, after he was dead, may easily be imagined; for had not all hands to toil, push, and groan over the getting of our cot back again? Resting when three parts of the ascent had been made, I mounted one of Dan O'Fee's famous "golden olive" flies, and at the very first cast up came a spanking ten pounder, as bright and clean as when he left the sea, and as the steel was driven home, away he went for the falls at racing speed. His first intention apparently was to try to get over the salmon ladder, but the pressure of seventy yards of line, in a wild race of water, brought him to his senses, and he was eventually got down on a short line and cleverly gaffed as the current bore him past the boat. Then came the celebration of those funereal rites,

PORTNA WEIR, KILREA.

Photo from G. Dallas, Coleraine.

which no angler dare disregard if he values either good sport or his own reputation. Pat Haggerty was the first to receive the sacremental cup, with which this majestic rite over a first fish is performed, and when Pat removed the vessel from his lips, he made a terrible grimace, as if he had taken poison in mistake, and gasping for breath, he exclaimed, "Ah! somebody's been spilin' that whuskey with water!" There was a roar of laughter, but Pat never recovered his good humour again that day, and I have fallen very low in his estimation through my use of water with the wine of the country. After much labour we got the unwieldy cot back into position, and, profiting by past experience, I set up a treble gut casting line, which would admit of holding a fish should he attempt to leave the weir pool, and rush into the wild water of the rapids. With the "golden olive" once more dancing in a deep eddy, a huge red fish rose, and immediately I was fast in a thirty pounder at least. For a moment only the fish hesitates about leaving his deep hole, and I hear Mike exclaim, "Murther! the baste! shure she's a back like our old sow." But I have not time to laugh, for with a terrific rush the "baste" is away down stream and pulling like a cart horse in the broken waters of the weir race. Fully eighty out of my hundred yards are already off the reel, and there is no earthly chance of the cot following, otherwise than along the bank, and the getting to shore in such wild water is a slow process. Holding on like grim death, with the rod bent double, I do my level best to turn the big fish, but it is hopeless, and presently the line goes with a bang, and I fall backward, with the rebound of the rod, and lay on the bottom of the boat unhurt, whilst Mike exhausts his vocabulary upon the lost fish. Winding up, we find that the treble gut has snapped like a pack thread, and we give up as I have no heart to cast another fly to-day. On the next two days I killed a single salmon each day, but let us pass them over, in order to tell you with what magnificent sport the week's fishing closed on Saturday. By the kind invitation of a gentleman whose hospitality I have enjoyed upon previous occasions in Ireland, I finished the week on five miles of the river, which is strictly preserved, and in which the heaviest of the late run fish make their breeding ground. This is the very choicest section of the Bann, and it yields some of the finest fish that are ever taken with rod and line in Ireland. Here is was that the son of my host and hostess—a smart lad, just home from Winchester—some years ago killed a grand forty pounder, after a fierce and desperate fight which lasted five hours. No more picturesque or delightfully-situated angler's home can be found in the United Kingdom than that occupied by my host.

Built on a ledge, apparently cut out of the hillside, the sloping ground to the water's edge is terraced, and the terraces are now aglow with autumn flowers, backed by hardy foliaged plants. From the little lawn, in front of the house, you look down upon the weir pool below. Southward from this elevated position the eye follows the course of the Bann, through a vista of rich timber trees whilst looking west, the blue mountains of Derry stand out clearly in the occasional gleams of autumn sunshine which light them up at intervals. My hostess is the most accomplished salmon angler in Ireland, and as she selects for me the killing fly for to-day, she declares that no more perfect fishing weather could be imagined—wind, water, and light are all that could be wished. And so myself and friend step into the boat, and commence to fish the fast water, on the ford below the weir—a "safe find," the boatman vowed. But never a touch did we get, and the cause was soon apparent. I had stuck to a "golden olive," instead of accepting the advice of the lady angler aforesaid. As we approached the next cast I put up the fly of her choice —one of Dan O'Fee's latest inventions—the famous "black and gold." And now the sport began. Arrived within two hundred yards of an eel weir my fly hangs a moment, there is a savage pull under water, and a flying leap of a twenty pounder revealed the fact that my fish was a new comer in splendid fighting condition. In wild rushes, and flying leaps, he went up stream at express speed, and thus avoided disturbing the water where he was hooked. Getting quickly to land I took up the running, and presently got on fighting terms with the fish. Once more he started a series of flying leaps. I could hear an accompaniment of wild "Whoroo's!" from the opposite bank, and a glance there showed that rascally boy Mike dancing and frantically waving his arms with excitement. But all my energies were needed to bring the fish to bank, and this was not done until my arms and back ached. Twenty-one and three-quarters of a pound, said the spring balance, and no more handsome fish ever fell to an angler's rod. Again we go back to the east, and in less than a quarter of an hour another big fish took the fly, this time the fight being much prolonged by reason of the hook pulling out of the salmon's mouth and catching in the gill cover. But why tell the whole story? The result of my six hours' fishing were five fish, which weighed respectively 21¾lb., 17½lb., 16lb., 14lb., and 11lb. Thus ended one of the best short day's fishing that I ever had, or am ever likely to have again, and but for my obstinacy in resisting the advice of a lady, as to the choice of a fly, the score would have been much heavier.

Did you ever do any night fishing for trout? Of course you did not, so come along with me to Portna weir, for we have got back to our fishing ground on the Bann, and rejoice in the quiet and repose of a comfortable farm house by the river-side. The modern name of a jaunting car is evidently a corruption of "jolting" car, which is by far the most appropriate title, as my weary bones can testify— but, let us go a-fishing. Rowing up, in the moonlight, we realize for the first time how low the river has run down, because, falling over this noble weir, some hundred yards wide, is only a thin stream of water instead of the tumbling mass whose roar could be heard in the village, two miles away. You will see by our illustration what Portna weir is like when the river is in good volume. The run of broken water from the foot of the weir is some 250 yards long, and it passes over large boulders, swirling into deep pools, where lie the cunning old trout who now only forsake their strongholds at night and range over the shallows in pursuit of food. A small boy, "Tommy," from the cabin close by, who kills more fish at this place than all the other anglers put together—wading to his armpits, wielding his rod and casting his flies in the eddying water and threading his way about the apron of the weir with perfect safety—this wee gossoon has confided to me that the big trout can only be caught by moonlight now. Three pounders, and even four pounders, have been captured of late by "Tommy," whilst he counts his two pound victims by the score—all taken by fly about nine in the evening. This weir pool is a charming spot at any time, hemmed in, as it is, by a pine wood on one side, and a high belt of rocks on the other. A pleasant breeze gently ruffles the surface of the stream, and the new moon sheds a gentle light upon the waters, reflecting in them the shadows of the trees and rocks, whilst the soft music of the fall keeps up a soothing lullaby. We have been waiting some time for evidence that the trout were beginning to feed, and now a circling ring here and there on the pool tells that supper has commenced. The tit-bit I furnish as my contribution to the feast is a medium sized "Turkey Brown," tied on the finest natural gut, and attached to a winch line long enough to kill a salmon. I am a strong believer in fine tackle. Whether or not these wary old rascals are inclined towards Turkey for a supper remains to be seen, but here goes the line of invitation. A hungry half-pounder is the first to accept, and he pays the penalty with his life, then several other victims follow, of three times the size, and presently there comes a heavy tug and the winch is whizzing like a tinker's grindstone, whilst a "whacker" takes out line at racing speed, bending my little 10ft. rod into a half-circle. Happily there are fifty yards of reel-line on the winch, and before that limit has been reached, the trout turns up stream, tugging deep down as all heavy fish do, and then with a rush flinging himself into the air, causing my good henchman to exclaim: "Oh! the wicket dievel; him four poun' too!" My man was mistaken, the fish had not broken me, and he was now bearing away for the boiling pool beneath the fall in search of some boulder or other retreat to rid himself of the line which holds him in restraint. But the relentless rod turns his head down stream, and again he leaps high in the air, repeating the process several times in rapid succession, and then making a mighty rush down stream, until I fear he will run all the line out and smash me. Giving him the butt as hard as light tackle will bear, he comes up doggedly to close quarters, and after fifteen minutes' exciting contest he is lifted into the boat—a well-fed fish of 4lb. 2oz. To kill such a fish in fast water, on a 7oz. rod and fine gut is pronounced to be a creditable performance, and, having performed the pagan rites of imbibing certain decoctions, over the body of the slain, pipes are lighted, and we resume operations. Another "whopper" was played and lost, a couple of pounders were added to the basket, and then we dropped down stream, to supper and to bed.

Anglers staying at Kilrea, can fish several other trout rivers within easy reach, the best of these being the Maine. A mail car between Kilrea and Cullybackey runs morning and evening, and the driver will drop the fisherman on the river's bank and pick him up again, when his day's work is done. The distance is ten miles, fare half-a-crown, and the Maine is a charming river, running through pretty surroundings—an ideal trout stream. There are times when the tidal portion of the Bann itself contains lashins of sea-trout, and good fun is got by spinning for them, the worst part of this sport being that many fish break away, for they are tender-mouthed. There is a line of railway from Kilrea to Coleraine, so that anglers can run down for a change with very little expenditure of time or money, and Portrush and the Causeway are but a little distance further on. The river Bush, at Bushmills, is also worth a visit from anyone wanting a change from Bann. There is a flytier in the little village of Bushmills, who can put you in the way of getting sport. Another string to the angler's bow is Lough Neagh which can be fished by going up to Toom Bridge, where fair accommodation will be found, and if good luck attends you, one of the big lake trout may fall to your lot. I am not fond of lough fishing myself, and so have not had much personal experiences of the angling resources of Neagh; but that it holds leviathan trout I know full well, for I have seen them netted. The secret of the enormous size to which trout here attain is the presence in the loughs of myriads of "pollen," a very delicate little fish, which is classed as a freshwater herring and is very good eating.

SHANNON AT CASTLE CONNELL.—THE FERRY.

From photo by W. Lawrence, Dublin.

THE SHANNON.

Castleconnell is not only famous for its enormous salmon and its splendid fishing, but it also boasts the possession of the champion fly-caster of the world. This mighty little wielder of the salmon rod—Mr. J. Enright—is the son of the hostess of the only hotel which this picturesque and delightfully situated village possesses. A very comfortable little hostelry we found it, during the month which we spent beneath its roof, and Hostess Enright treated us to generous fare. Albeit the hotel charges were proportionately high, and I should scarcely recommend the Shannon fishing to a man of limited means. In spite of its great natural beauties, and all the advantages with which nature has endowed it, every thing about the place bears traces of poverty and decay. The village is placed upon the Limerick side of the river Shannon, which is here about two hundred yards wide; a rushing turbulent water, boiling over huge boulders and rocks which seek to impede its course. For a distance of about ten miles westward gentle hills, richly timbered, slope up on either side of the river's banks, and these hills are dotted at intervals with stately mansions once occupied by aristocratic families who have gone to ruin since the bad times came, and their tenants ceased to pay their rack rent. There are half a dozen such desolate palatial residences in sight, all shut up and going to decay. The tales told of their former tenants are pretty much the same in every case: fast living, open houses, and prodigal waste, so long as money could be got by hook or by crook. It is said that the last of these Irish aristocrats, who was "sold up" about three months ago, kept for her private use a stud of 20 horses, and she is credited with having wasted £30 000 within the past two years. In fact, to quote the language of my informant, "she went to the Devil in fine style, and cheated the Banks into the bargain!" The loss of the resident gentry has seriously affected the prosperity of the locality, but the villagers have taken the parks for grazing at rents averaging 40s. an acre; and it is estimated that each acre will fatten a bullock. I said just now that the village of Castleconnell had about it signs of decay, but the extent to which it has suffered from the bad times may be gathered from the fact that whereas the population, forty years ago, was 1,000, it is now only 350! The village High-street is barely 200 yards long, and to provide for the refreshment of its 350 inhabitants, there are, in that short distance, eleven fully licensed houses for the sale of intoxicants, and it is fair to assume that they, as well as emigration, have contributed towards reducing the population. When I expressed my astonishment at this superfluity of shebeens my boatman said there were three shebeens which had recently shut up. Did the magistrates take the licenses away? "Not a bit of it" says he. "It was a new curate who came into the parish, formed a temperance league, and ruined the drink trade entirely." Did many people join? Indeed they did—more than half the parish took the pledge—and made the drinksellers awfully mad—they could not obtain enough profit to pay for their licenses.

But enough of these wretched drink troubles, let us throw them aside and go on tramp together from our delightful little village of Castleconnell to the historical City of Limerick. The distance is variously stated by all to whom we appeal for information, but, assuming, as I always do, that an Irish mile is a mile and a quarter full, the journey can be performed within three hours on foot. For the first few miles, the road is bounded on either side by massive stone walls, whilst continuous rows of beech trees interlace their branches overhead, thus forming a natural arch, through which the sunlight plays, producing a long vista of light and shade that is exceedingly beautiful. The walls are overgrown with ferns, lichens, and moss, which here flourish in as much luxuriance as if they were cultivated with all the care and skill that money can command. A most delightful country lane, the like of which I have never seen before, but the music of the Shannon can be heard in the valley below, and it is very vexing that this fern-covered wall prevents our catching glimpses of the river between the trees. You can have too much of a good thing, and I confess to a feeling akin to relief when we eventually emerge from that long avenue, which has occupied an hour's smart walking.

Presently we come to a road bridge which spans the Mulcaire River, which empties itself into the Shannon close by. This little river teems with mighty trout, which work up from the Shannon, and it is also a favourite stream with the grilse, who turn into it on their run up from the sea. Foregathering with a local angler, who is "worming for trouts," he tells me that the fishing in the Mulcaire is free. So little is it preserved that poaching is carried on extensively by the "boys." This description of the poachers has no limit with regard to age, because a hoary-headed old sinner, with one foot in the grave would be called a "boy" if he went poaching. I was very much impressed with the beauty and fishing possibilities of this turbulent little river, and I promised myself the pleasure of some day testing its angling merits. This promise I hope yet to redeem.

Away down the main road to Limerick—a road eighty feet wide—we pass through the village of Newcastle, and approach the city; and nothing more squalid and filthy than the cabins which flank this thoroughfare could be found in Ireland. Wretched hovels, with heaps of manure and slush at their doors, ducks, goats, and pigs grubbing in search of offal, liquid manure running across the paths into the road, mud-begrimed, half-naked children, women in rags and tatters—these are the sights which first greet us as we approach the city of the broken treaty. Nor does a nearer approach dispel the first impression. We enter by way of Clare-street, which consists of enormous houses, four and five stories high, bearing evidences of a past prosperity, but now reduced to abject poverty. Along by the river side we pick our way, amongst pools of slush, filth, and garbage that would put to blush the dirtiest slum of an Asiatic city, and make our way to the principal street which Limerick boasts. We must, of course, go to Cruez's hotel, and there present our credentials from that fiery patriot, Father Kelly. Although for historical interest Limerick has a history second to no city in the United Kingdom, yet few relics of its famous past survive. King John's castle is in a ruinous state, but enough remains to show what a noble Norman stronghold it was, with its seven massive towers and high walls of vast strength and thickness. The stone on which the famous treaty of capitulation of 1791 was signed stands on a pedestal by the river side, and, having seen this, and looked over the cathedral, we shall have exhausted the lions of the place. The chief characteristics of Limerick are high houses and dirt—the back streets literally reek with filth. The return journey can be done by rail—two trains each day—and the distance traversed, fifteen miles, is covered, on an average in a trifle under the hour—not bad work, that, for travelling on an Irish branch line.

The fishing at Castleconnell may be said to commence at the World's End weir, and to end at the Doonas Falls. Within the recollection of living men, this two miles of water was free to all comers—so say the local Hampdens—but the adjoining owners of the soil have for years asserted their riparian rights, and fabulous rents for the fishing are now obtained.

Our illustration shows the New Garden salmon pool, which is but a hundred yards from the hotel door, and this pool is about the centre of the Castleconnell fishing. The old man, in the foreground of the picture, is the blind ferryman, Dan Enright. He was, in his day, one of the best boatmen on the Shannon, but he lost his eyesight through the branch of an overhanging tree striking him in the face. Across the fierce stream of the river, to and fro, he plies, guiding his cot into a little bay cut out of the bank on either side, with unerring accuracy, and earning a

miserable pittance from the poor country folk who are his scanty customers. He was a very old man when I last saw him, and his recollections of famous men and women who had fished at Castleconnell, or been attracted there by the sylvan beauties of the place, are very entertaining, but, if you listened to them, you must be prepared to be told at the end that your entertainer was as poor as Lazarus. Poor old Dan, I pity you from my very soul in your life of perpetual darkness, and admire your christian spirit of resignation and thankfulness, that has in it no shade of repining. "I used to grieve," the old man said, "when the spring came and I heard the boys tell how they had taken, may be, a thirty-five pounder on our water and me not seen it—but the Lord's will be done." Old Dan's post, when waiting customers, is close beside the famous ruins of an old castle built by one of the O'Brien's, king of Munster. This stronghold, perched high upon a huge pedestal of natural rock—and only approachable by a narrow path hewn out of the side—overlooks the river, and in the wars of William and James the strength of this fortress gave great trouble to the besiegers. Now let us follow the path by the river side down about a short mile to the rapids of Doonas, and you must confess that such a magnificent sight is worth a 500 mile journey.

The accompanying illustration will convey some slight idea of this turbulent rapid where, hemmed in on both sides by rocky banks and overhanging trees, the river rushes in a foaming cataract for the length of a quarter of a mile, the enormous body of water pouring over huge masses of rock which impede its progress, and the noise of the rushing flood can be heard at a considerable distance. Lady Massy owns the adjacent land—an aged lady, living a solitary life, in a house falling to pieces with decay. In the midst of this tumbling cataract is a smooth piece of water behind a stupendous mass of rock, and in this slack water the salmon in their upward passage sometimes rest. This rock will be seen in our third illustration of the pool below Doonas fall. To kill a salmon on that rock tests to the utmost the skill of an angler, but it is done occasionally, and the man who accomplishes it may fairly claim to have established his right to be considered a master of the art.

I was very unfortunate in my choice of a visit to Castleconnell, for the fishing was rascally bad, to say the least of it, and this was aggravated by the tricks of the people at the Killaloe weir. Some works were there in progress, and the waters rose and fell several feet in the course of each day. None the less my month on the Shannon was a very pleasant one, and as a holiday it was very enjoyable. Fishing from a shallow cot, held in the fast, broken water by two men— one at stem and the other at the starn—armed with iron-shod punt poles is not easy work, and, truth to tell, the uneasy motion of the boat made my chum sea-sick, to begin with. The sight of huge salmon, from 20lb. to 30lb., rising in mid-stream, was too tempting to be resisted, and go for them he would, and did, regardless of "mal de mer." In the early part of the season, six inch blue phantom minnows account for most of the Shannon salmon, or big yellow flies, the size of a canary bird, containing about 10s. worth of gold pheasant toppings, are the correct thing. The water is so fast that the fly fishes itself and requires no "working," but cutting the flies (trailing) is a method much in vogue on this river.

Our illustrations show three sections of the Shannon, from the pool opposite the village, down to the easy water below the Doonas falls.

SHANNON—DOONAS FALLS.

From photo by W. Lawrence, Dublin.

THE DARENTH—EYNSFORD POOL.

From photo by R. B. Lodge, Enfield.

THE DARENTH.

This pretty little trout stream has its source at Westerham, in a small lake upon the "Squerries" estate. Thence it flows through Brasted Sundridge, Riverhead, Otford, Shoreham, Eynsford, Farningham, and Horton Kirby, eventually discharging into the estuary of the Thames at Dartford. Various tributary springs help to swell the volume of this little river, the principal contributions being derived from Brasted, Riverhead, Bradbourne Ponds, and Greatness Farm, in the lower end of Sevenoaks. Having regard to its size, there is no trout river in England so prolific as the Darenth. And it is equally true that in no river, of my acquaintance, are the trout so highly educated! I have fished this Queen of southern trout streams for fully thirty years, and I love every turn of the happy valley through which it flows. Thirty years is a big span to look back upon, and many men have come and gone in that period whose names and faces were once familiar as anglers on the Darenth. In that period, too, the various lengths of water that once were accessible have one by one been closed against the public and fancy rents are commanded for every scrap of fishing right now obtainable. The only open portions of the river that can now be fished, by day tickets, are at Dunton Green Mill, the "Plough" water, at Eynsford, the "Lion," at Farningham, and the "Fighting Cocks," at Horton Kirby. Upon the principle that no trout fishing is bad, only some is better than others, I offer no expression of opinion as to the sport which anyone is likely to get for their half-crowns on these day ticket waters. There are some two or three exclusive clubs whose members possess the enviable right to fish certain well-stocked sections of the Darenth, but they would not thank me for going into details. Suffice it, the Darenth fishing is becoming—indeed it has become—an expensive luxury, which is no longer within the reach of anyone save those blessed with long purses.

If I have taken heavy toll from the Darenth—and I own to a basket of ten brace weighing 38lb.—yet have I made ample and handsome restitution to the stream, in the way of restocking. For every fish that I have taken out of our little river I have certainly put ten into it. This is the only way in which a good head of trout can be maintained in a stream so heavily fished, where ducks, swans, pike, and herons work their wicked wills upon the redds and amongst the young fry. I said something, in the foregoing, about the fine size and quality of the Darenth trout, and in proof of this assertion I may point to the fact that two trout have been captured within recent times—between Eynsford and Farningham — weighing respectively $4\frac{3}{4}$lbs. and 8lbs. 11ozs. They both died ignominious and inglorious deaths, at the hands of rustic poachers, but that fact is not recorded upon the glass cases in which they are enshrined.

Before passing away from the question of keeping up the stock of fish in our Kentish trout stream, let me say a word or two upon the havoc wrought of late years upon its trout by the pike. The Darenth is infested with pike, and the sooner this terrible fact is brought home to the upper riparian owners, the greater will be the chances of ridding the river of these pests. We are on the eve of the spawning season, and some concerted efforts are necessary to secure the gravid pike and thus prevent them reproducing their species. Up to some six or seven years ago, no one ever heard of a jack being seen in this charming trout stream. There is no mystery surrounding the introduction of "Esox lucius." A pond, fed by springs at the source of the river in Westerham, maintained a few trout, but they did badly, the flow of water being very small. Some clever person persuaded the owner to put pike in the water, and he, knowing nothing of the habits of the "varmint," acted on the advice thus given. In three years the progeny of these imported pike had escaped from the pond, dropped down stream, and distributed themselves along fully fifteen miles of the river ! Pike from six to eight pounds apiece are now common throughout the whole course of the Darenth, and there are no end of smaller specimens—every holding pool has some of them. Unless a war of extermination is declared against these creatures, trout fishing on the Darenth will be utterly and irretrievably ruined. To run a net through deep pools here and there, once in the season, killing from fifteen to twenty pike, is all very well, but it is utterly insufficient and I appeal to the riparian owners and tenants of club waters to take up this question and do all that can be done by an unrelenting war to rid the Darenth of these vermin. What they will do in the way of damage to the trout is well exemplified by what has recently occurred within my own knowledge. A small back stream—no larger than a small ditch—and not a hundred yards long, contained a goodly stock of yearling trout. They were nice fish, ranging from six to seven inches long, and with the autumn floods they would, no doubt, have gone down to increase the stock in the river. But a wretched little pike, scarcely two pounds in weight, found his way into the nursery, and before his presence was discovered, the whole of the young stock were devoured! When killed, this hungry pikelet had in his pouch a trout nearly one quarter of a pound weight ! To me, these facts are a source of deep concern, because I foresee that, failing prompt and vigorous action, trout fishing on the Darenth will be ruined. Artificial re-stocking may do something to counteract the ravages of the pike, but it is hopeless work to go on putting young trout in for these rapacious savages to eat. The recent floods have cleared the weed beds away, and a net could now be run through the river with ease. Why not do it? In a short length of less than half a mile of the Darenth five pike have been snared ranging from four pounds to eight pounds, in a few weeks ; and this fact is of itself, a strong proof that the state of affairs is indeed serious. For myself this condition of things is a source of grave anxiety, for I have done all that in me lies to increase the stock of trout, and improve the sport of those favoured anglers who are privileged to fish the Darenth. But all our efforts in the direction of re-stocking are wasted, so long as the young trout are devoured by the insatiable pike. A war of extermination against the common enemy is necessary, and it must be persistently maintained and unceasingly waged, if the sport of the trout angler on the Darenth is to be kept up in the future.

Another serious enemy to the trout in this stream are the herons. They are not numerous, but so sure as you turn in a lot of yearlings on some shallows, so surely will a heron make those shallows his feeding ground. Where these birds come from is a mystery, because we have no heronry anywhere in the Darenth valley, so far as I am aware of. For weeks past we have been sorely troubled by the number of dead fish, upon the shallows of our Eynsford club water. But last Sunday morning I caught sight of the culprit—a huge heron standing knee-deep in the stream. I am not sure that a heron has got a knee, but that does not matter. This big bird flopped up clumsily, and, rising to a great height, sailed away over the hills to the west. I propose to save him the necessity of catching his own trout in future, by baiting some rabbit gins with small fish.

Kingfishers, like the herons, find their way to our trout nurseries, and what is more they come to stop, when they find their larder well stored. I know of three kingfishers nests upon our length of the Darenth this season, and I would not have them interfered with on any account. They take toll of the trout fry, no doubt, but they eat more minnows than trout, and I do not begrudge them their share of our fish.

What has always astonished me is the fact that none of the Kentish riparian owners have ever gone in for artificial trout breeding. The needful apparatus cost next to nothing and, given a constant supply of water, nature will do the rest. I once turned a thousand Loch Leven yearlings into the Eynsford length of this river, and they grew rapidly to half pound fish, retaining their white silvery appearance quite distinct from the Darenth brown trout. But when their third year came we had a big push of water down, and everyone of those Loch Levens went away with it to the sea. I know very well that some of my angling, naturalist friends will say that these Leven trout became assimilated to the native trout and thus became indistinguishable. It is an ingenious theory, but it will not hold water; because I and others are able to fix the period of migration, and to prove that some of these fish were captured in the eel traps as they went away to the sea. I am not prepared to deny that Loch Levens when crossed with common brown trout, lose their distinctive characteristics, but once a pure Loch Leven, always a Loch Leven.

Since the construction of the Darenth Valley main drainage system—with its outfall sewer laid beside the course of the river—there has been a marked decrease in the volume of water in the stream. This has, in turn, affected the fishing prejudicially, by making the trout more shy and difficult to approach, upon the shallows. In fact some of the best spots, in former times, are no longer worth fishing over, as there is no longer water enough to cover anything larger than a yearling. It must not be imagined, however, from these foregoing remarks, that I consider our charming little trout stream is in a bad way. On the contrary, it is well stocked with very fine trout, and my only desire is to stimulate those who fish it, to each do something towards keeping up the reputation of the Darenth.

With regard to the best killing flies on this river, if I was condemned to select and use only one pattern my choice would be a blue-winged, ginger-hackled, quill-bodied, gnat. But as I am not so restricted in choice, my fly-box contains some fifty stock patterns, to say nothing of fancy productions. One of the most curious things about the Darenth flies is that you may have a run of unprecedented luck on some particular fly, which will be taken greedily by the trout for a whole season. And then you will never see another counterpart of this fly for two or three years. This is true of the big olive duns, the whirling blues, primrose yellow duns putty-coloured ephemera. Gravel-beds were, at one time, the commonest of our early flies, on all the shallow, gravelly bottomed lengths of the river. But I have not seen a single living specimen upon this stream for the past three years. No doubt these mysterious disappearances are due to the hatch-out of flies being killed off by frosty nights. There is no royal road to the selection of the right fly for this river, but the angler should endeavour to match the insects upon which the trout are feeding. Taking the months in their order I should recommend the following:—

April.—Dark, medium, and pale olives, whirling blues, claret spinners, and March browns.

May.—Iron blues, black gnats, grey quills, and alders, during the day, and govenors for the evening rise.

June.—May-fly, as long as it lasts, yellow duns, blue winged, badger hackle midges, and small soldier palmers, in addition to any of the other flies that may be seen upon the water.

July and August.—Pale watery olives, tail-to-tail midges, grey quill, with flat silver body and badger hackle, red quill, with gold body, for use in bright sunshine. These flat tinselled bodied flies are very effective in a blazing sunshine on a perfectly calm and glassy surface when the "sky is of copper and the river of brass." Red spinners, brown sedges, and silver-ribbed white moths, may be added to govenors for the evening rise.

As to the size of flies, No. 0 is the most useful, after the first month of the season, but the flies for evening fishing should be dressed on No. 1 hooks. I do not profess to have given an exhaustive list in the foregoing, but the angler who fishes the Darenth with the flies named will not go far wrong.

Too much stress cannot be put upon the absolute necessity of using fine tackle for the water is so shallow and bright that it is waste of time to cast over fish with coarse gut. I use the very finest natural gut down to the three last links and these taper from x to xx and xxx drawn at the tip. My gut casts are never longer than 4ft. 6in. long, and I tie my own, but I occasionally use two links of xxx at point when casting over very shy fish.

So much by way of introduction. It was not my intention originally to attempt any such instruction in the art of catching Darenth trout, but the foregoing has been written in the hope that it may prove useful.

MAY FLY ON DARENTH.

The May-fly season upon the Darenth is supposed to begin on the Saturday before Whit-Monday, but the rise of fly has, up to the time of writing this note, been very small, and the trout have taken it badly. I am located in our angling hut, on the banks of the Darenth, and I have therefore been able to keep my eye on the river through all the hours of daylight. As a matter of fact I am completing my book, "Angling Holidays," amidst these congenial surroundings, and I am sandwiching in some May-fly fishing between the spells of grinding out "copy." What are the exact proportions of fishing and work, it is not necessary to specify. The other evening, I was full of good resolutions; came in at sunset, hung up the rod, brewed myself a jorum of tea, and ate a Robinson Crusoe meal. My companion for the day went away to town, taking the day's catch with him. Yes, I really would put in a square six hours' work. And at it I went with a dogged determination—for fully ten minutes ! Then I remembered there was nothing but a very stale lump of bread and some butter for breakfast ! Moreover, the evening was deliciously calm and warm, and there was not a breath of wind stirring. The air was laden with the perfume of hawthorn, the river looked very inviting, and there was a rascally old trout of my acquaintance, down at the first bend of the stream, not a hundred yards away ! It really was a shame to shut oneself up in the hut on such an evening, and—well I yielded to temptation ! But that trout at the corner was sucking in black gnats, and paid not the slightest attention to my May-fly when placed a few inches in front of his nose. He evidently knew the pattern. Nor would he respond to any of the lines of invitation which I sent him, including an exact imitation of the wee

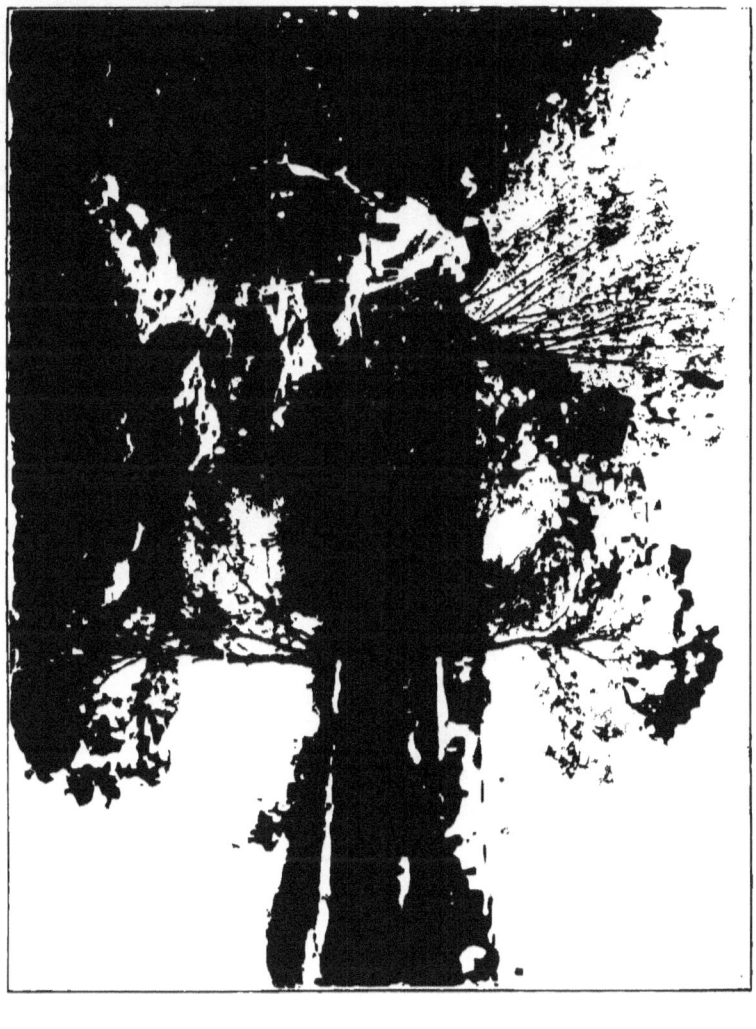

DARENTH—THE AUTHOR AT WORK.

insect upon which he was feeding. The light was still good enough to enable him to see fine silkworm gut to which the fly was attached. To sit on a bank, smoke a pipe of peace, and listen to the nightingales, is not a bad way of waiting for the light to fade. In the gloaming I dropped a large "governor" at the right spot, and the trout took it with a sousing rise immediately. I had no end of a fight with him, for he was feeding on the edge of a big willow branch with a lot of floating weeds attached to it. Truth to tell he got into the fringe of this haven of safety in spite of all I could do to keep him out. But he tore the lump of weeds away eventually, and I fought it out with him thus enveloped in a mass of green stuff! None the less he eventually gave up the unequal contest, and proved to be a handsome, well-fed fish, of fully 1¾lb. avoirdupois—not fisherman's—weight. And what a breakfast he made, both for myself and our man Friday.

The corn crakes are very numerous in our valley this year, and a pair of these birds are breeding within sight of my bedroom window. By the aid of a powerful glass I watched their movements and saw the old cock-bird run about amongst the grass jerking his head from side to side, uttering "crakes" as he did so. The direction of the bird's head as each "crake" was given produced the ventriloquial effect of making the call appear to come from different quarters. The old birds leave us usually, on their autumn migration, early in August, whilst the youngsters, if a late brood, remain quite a month longer in the meadows where they are hatched. These birds, to look at, appear to be quite incapable of a long-sustained flight, and they seldom go more than a couple of hundred yards when flushed by the partridge shooters. It is placed beyond all doubt, however, that in their annual migrations, spring and autumn, these short-winged crakes not only cross the Channel, but they sometimes cover more than a hundred miles without alighting. There is nothing connected with natural history which possesses so much interest to the student as the migration of birds, and yet how little we know upon the subject! We hail their arrival as the harbingers of spring, and regret their departure as the first signs of approaching winter; but whence they come or whither they go is, for the most part, mere guess work. It is true that we no longer believe in the old fable—which perplexed Gilbert White when he wrote his charming "History of Selborne"—that the swallows burrowed and "slumbered" during the winter months. But we have yet much to learn on this fascinating subject of migration of birds, and the man who brings our knowledge upon this point "up to date" will make an enduring name for himself.

Did you ever see a blackbird attack a cat? I have been greatly interested in contests of this kind, which go on at various periods of the day before the window at which I am writing. There is a blackbird's nest, with young in it, in one tree, and in another hollow elm-pollard—not six feet away from the nestlings—our Man Friday's cat has a kitten. Cats do not, as a rule, breed in the holes of trees, as you know. But this cat is not as other cats are; she is in no sense domesticated. There is no male cat, that we know of, within a very long distance—but that is another story. Our cat kittened in an old disused barn, to begin with, and her numerous progeny were no sooner born than she began to provide for their sustenance. A couple of leverets were amongst the tit-bits which she brought home, and every hedge-row was robbed of its callow broods and sitting wild birds. I am a long time getting to her fights with the cock blackbird, but that will come in presently. Well, those kittens were, with one exception, killed in the interests of sport. The mother cat considered the matter of her bereavement carefully over for a whole day, and at night she took prompt action. The surviving kitten disappeared, and this is where the blackbird comes in. He besieged the hiding place of the old cat and her baby, puffing his feathers out like a broody hen, raising his back hair, and using the most violent language of which a blackbird is capable. Eventually Mrs. Tabby resented this disturbance, and came out of her hole. The bird swooped round her in circles, as she slowly

THE CLUB COTTAGE, ON DARENTH.

descended the trunk of the tree backwards, dashing at her whenever there was a chance of doing so without risk. This was the beginning of the fight, and it has since gone on every day, whenever the cat shows herself. Even when she is lying asleep on the ground, in the sun, Master Blackie sits on a post close by and reviles her, and sometimes he hops around her in a circle with as much fierceness as a game cock, uttering fierce notes of defiance. The cat makes occasional dashes at him, and eventually settles down and pretends to ignore him. But she is on the pounce, all the time, and I much fear that Master Blackie will presently lose his life in one of these encounters.

The accompanying illustration of "An Angler's Hut on the Darenth" is the headquarters of our small club; and the "Man Friday" is there shown, reproaching us for being late for lunch. No man is a hero to his valet; and "Friday" has no sympathy with the folly of men who will linger beyond the meal hour over a rising trout, that won't take, and let chops and potatoes get cold.

Trout fishing has in our Kentish valley greatly improved within the past two weeks—thanks to the warmer nights —and some very fine bags have been made. The Darenth is very low and bright, but with gossamer gut and small flies the trout have taken freely. I killed the "Darenth Ghost" last Saturday. A perfectly white trout, save for the spots which are common to all his family. We have known the "Ghost" for the past three years, his habitat being limited to about 60 yards of the river—with a deep pool at either end. Some mention of this fish made by me in print brought a long and learned letter from a German professor to an angling paper. He proved to his own entire satisfaction that the "Ghost" was blind. That the loss of colour was due to the loss of eyesight, entailing a consequent failure in the secretion of certain pigments which furnish the external colourings of trout. We were all deeply impressed by the learning of the professor, and asked him to tell us some more. But when I spotted the "Ghost" last Saturday, in the upper pool of his territory, he was behaving in a very strange manner for a blind fish.

Except for the assurances of that learned professor, I could have sworn that the "Ghost" was "smutting." That is sucking in microscopic black flies, no bigger than the head of a pin. Whatever pleasure or profit trout derive from this "smutting" is one of the angling problems which no man as yet has been able to solve. I put a lovely Alder about a foot in front of the "Ghost's" nose, and he examined the fly critically, opened his mouth longingly, and then, with a sweep of his tail, sheered off. Blind was he, my learned professor? Not much! Whatever may have caused his skin to blanch—the trout's, not the professor's—it was not lack of eyesight. This was a rude shock to my belief in that eminent German savant, and I thought the matter out, over a pipe, with one eye on the "Ghost." Then I laid siege to him again and three different flies were presented at intervals for his inspection and rejected. So I gave up the "Ghost" for a time and plied my craft successfully amongst his more confiding friends and relations. But the persons who regulate the waters at mills appear to take a satanic delight in making things unpleasant for Saturday anglers. All the accumulated garbage of the past week is sent down for his delectation; the water is shut off, reducing the stream to a mere trickle, and sending the trout scuttling to the pools. Then the hatches are lifted, and down comes another avalanche of weeds and rubbish. It is a wholesome chastening of the Job-like patience of an angler, is a Saturday afternoon on the Darenth. But when, at length, the evil genii of the river had worked their wicked will, to their full content, and had gone home to tea, I returned to my post, beneath the willow, and again interviewed the "Ghost." He was still hard at it, upon those "smuts" and I offered him a microscopic midge, tied on a piece of gut as fine as a human hair. The "Ghost" sailed up to it, sucked in the tempting morsel—without the slightest hesitation—and then we fought it out in that pool! He had different ideas to mine, as to how that fight should be conducted. His view was that by getting down out of the pool, into the shallow below, the friendly weeds, and a couple of stranded eel traps, might save his life. But it was not to be; he made a gallant fight for it, and finally came to net without a wag left in his tail. And this was the inglorious end of the "Ghost," concerning whose blindness I should like to hear further from that deeply learned and eminent German professor! The "Ghost" has a piebald brother -- but that is another story.

The treacherous month of May having fully sustained its reputation, has now given place to the leafy month of June, and the mystic words "The fly is up" have gone the round of the angling world; yes "she" is up in her myriads, and whatever may be urged against the wholesale slaughter of trout, which goes on during the "duffers' carnival," there is something to be said on the other side of the question. For my own part, I defend May-fly fishing upon the ground that it enables you to clear out some of the big fish that never rise to a fly at any other time, and who live upon trout fry all the rest of the year. But I am not concerned about the ethics of fishing with artificial drake; my present purpose is rather to invite you to share with me the first day's "May-flying" on the Darenth in this year of grace. The ungenial weather and cold winds have kept back the delicate "ephemera vulgata," and retarded their hatching to the extent of a week beyond the date of their usual appearance on our queen of Kentish trout streams; but we shall find them up in goodly numbers when presently the sun has warmed the waters. By the kindness of a generous non-angling owner, we have to-day the run of a lovely length of the river which is seldom fished, and we are specially enjoined by our host to "thin the ranks of those big fellows, and don't spare them." At the outset our prospects of doing this are not very promising, for the day is yet young, and not a sign of insect life can we discover upon the calm surface of the stream. Let us be patient, as becomes the true disciples of old Isaac Walton, for assuredly there is abundant material in this delightful Kentish valley wherewith to occupy our time until the trout begin to feed. How lovely and fresh, in their delicate spring tints, do the trees and hedgerows look, and the rich pastures are aglow with kingcups and wild hyacinth, whilst the air is laden with the perfume of May blossom.

> "How little dream the crowd
> 'Midst the city's tumult loud,
> How much pure and soothing bliss
> May be found in scenes like this."

The man who could wander by the Darenth side on such a morning as this without being impressed with the natural beauties of his surroundings must be a curmudgeon unworthy of our gentle craft. You and I, my friend, sitting on a fallen tree, and smoking a matutinal pipe — for no saints are we — look about us and declare that, in spite of the sin, sorrow, and misery which afflict mankind, the world is still as fresh and beautiful as when our first parents gazed upon it in the Garden of Eden. That happy mother water hen, with her tiny brood of dabchicks paddling around her in the sunny nook yonder, by the bed of wild iris, is one of the prettiest sights we have seen for a long time, and we presently turn our attention to a baby waterrat breakfasting on the bank within a few yards of us. What a dainty young rascal it is, and what airs he gives himself, as, between the courses, he performs his morning toilet quite oblivious of our presence! Was that a trout which caused the splash in the pool, beneath the old overhanging pollard? No, a flash of turquoise blue, and another splash in the stream shows very plainly that a kingfisher is breakfasting. We will not begrudge him his meal, for he is one of the few scarce birds of Kent that has survived the brutal instinct of extermination which prompts "Velveteens" to kill anything and everything that is rare. Here come the scouts of the May-fly army, and these stragglers show that the "rise" will soon begin, so let us catch one of the "green drake" and do our best to find an artificial fly to match him, as we saunter leisurely to the sheltered stretch of water where the fish rise earliest. These May-flies are creatures of slow growth, remaining a whole year (some people say two years) under water before they attain to a perfect state; a gauze-winged beautiful

insect, which flutters out its brief existence in but a few hours, changing in that brief span from olive green to snowy whiteness, with jet black appendages. Truly, the history and metamorphoses of this fly are the most marvellous of the many marvels of the insect world. We will move on to the deep water, which is the stronghold of these big trout that we are especially enjoined to wage war upon. Here, in this bend of the river, on a memorable occasion, I killed a brace of three-pounders, and that there are others of equal weight is not open to doubt. Judging from the "boils" one sees, the fish are feeding on the May-fly, under water—intercepting it as it rises from the river bed—and this requires a style of fishing which is not very congenial to the dry-fly man. With Ogden's "Gem," tied hackle fashion, the fly is easily pulled under water when fished up stream and it is far and away more deadly in this form than when dangled down stream in the "chuck-and-chance-it" fashion. A big tail out of water and the rod bent double proclaim the fact that the May-fly battle has begun, and a right royal fight it is, for a seven-ounce split cane rod is but a feeble weapon to be used against trout of aldermanic proportions. Fighting deep down, and boring steadily up stream, the fish appears to be going to give in easily, but suddenly, without a wink of warning, he bolts down stream, like a flash of lightning, and is entangled in a loose bush on the shallows before we can realise the situation. But the bush is too small to afford him a dead pull, and he tows it about and tugs at it fiercely until, worn out with the unequal contest, he is scooped out, a splendid Darenth trout of two and three-quarter pounds. The fly is now coming down thickly, and the trout give over "bulging" and come to the surface to feed. We quickly increase our score and reach a rude footbridge of timber, where a good fish is found sucking in the fly as they eddy round in the swirl of a post on the up-stream side of this clumsy old structure. Yes, "He's got it," you exclaim, but he has bolted under the arch, and is twenty yards away down stream, fighting desperately for a weed bed ! Oh ! for a good twelve-footer, with plenty of backbone in it ; these seven-ounce rods are a mistake for May-fly work. But I stick to my fish, and hold him all I dare, and we can see him below the bridge, lashing round, and floundering about in a manner which betokens that he is nearly done for. Come up stream he will not, and with my line through the arch of that wretched bridge the chances of bringing the fish to net are strongly against me. But the cast is a good one (never use drawn gut for May-fly), and if the hook does not draw the case is by no means hopeless. All attempts to drive the fish up stream and through the arch proved fruitless, and to follow him is impossible, for the water beneath the bridge is five feet deep. When finally he gave up the struggle, and lay like a log on the water, I drove the spike of my rod into the ground, fastened the winch line, and —by dint of getting wet to my waist—put the net beneath him, and out he came ! A lovely two-pounder, with a bloom upon him like a peach, and bejewelled with spots as brilliant as rubies. And yet there are people who will tell you there is no variety in angling, and that the catching of one trout is but a repetition of the "same old story." The sun has begun to sink away westward, the basket is heavy, and so we cry a halt and count the slain. A noble show they make : eight brace all told, the smallest, one and three-quarter pounds, and the best, two and three-quarter pounds. We admire them greatly, indeed we perform those pagan rites over them which tradition sanctions, and, although the day is still young, we cry, "Hold enough !"

In the making of artificial May-flies, and the "invention" of new patterns there is no end ; but Ogden's hackled "gem" has, in our experience, no equal, either as a floater or when fished sunk. With this fly we killed our "record" basket of ten brace of trout, weighing 38lbs., in a deep, slow running river, fishing dry. Early rising for May-fly angling is a mistake, as the "rise" seldom comes on sufficiently strong to bring the big trout up until the sun has warmed the water, and aired the valley. You only fag yourself unnecessarily, by commencing too soon, and make a toil of what would otherwise have been a day of pleasure. Acting upon this principle we commenced operations one day this week at noon, in a lovely length of the Darenth valley, which shall be nameless, for obvious reasons. The cold north-east wind was tempered by a hot sun, and these conditions are always the most favourable on the river in question. Whatever may have been the case, when the old song originated about

" When the wind is in the south,
It blows the bait in fishes' mouth."

Such has never been our experience. With a cross-stream wind, the flies drifted close to the opposite bank, and the feeding fish were all there, sucking them in as they came down. We were limited to five brace, and as there are plenty of big trout in the waters, we make it a point of honour to put back all but well-fed fish that are over a pound apiece. To kill small trout with a May-fly is unsportsmanlike, and should be strongly discountenanced. The chief charm of this fishing is to get hold of the big fellows, who seldom rise to a fly at any other time; and to accomplish this we pass all the shallows, and only fish the deep pools and the eddies formed by projecting alder stumps. From such a stronghold came our first really good fish, and he took the fly, making only a dimple on the surface of the water. But a wild dash up stream followed the strike, and then he came back with a rush to his old quarters, boring into the alder stump, but vainly endeavouring to foul the cast. After a stubborn fight in the deep water, away he went down stream, making for a weedy shallow below, but he never reached it, and the little seven-ounce split cane rod won the unequal battle, for the gallant two-pounder was laid quivering upon the grass. A broad belt of trees shelters us from the wind, and the sun makes himself felt, so we go back to the deep water, smoke the pipe of peace, and wait for signs of another big fish. The swallows are busy amongst the May-fly, swooping down upon them as they float by on the surface of the stream, and seizing them with a snap of the beak, that can be heard

where we sit, the wood-pigeons coo softly in the trees, and the wandering voice of the cuckoo comes down from the wood above,
"At once far off and near."

It is a mistake, when May-fly fishing, to hurry over good water, that you know holds large fish. They rise fitfully, as a rule, but when you have marked one down, lay siege to him, and you will get him eventually, provided you understand your business. There was a big boil in the middle of the slow running pool, a few minutes ago, and we have mounted a new hackled "gem," carefully anointing it with vaseline, to increase its buoyancy. Taking advantage of a passing cloud over the sun, the tempting morsel of wood-duck and steel is dropped a couple of feet above the spot where the fish rose; and he takes it with a bold head and tail rise, like that of a salmon. Down he goes, like a submerged barge, when he feels the hook, boring about on the bottom, and making nasty snatches on the line, that are very trying to a light rod; but this wee bit of split cane has killed a grilse in its day, and who's afraid? Giving him all the butt we dare, the trout is kept moving. He has notions of his own as to the best methods of defence, and stubborn resistance is the policy that commends itself to his judgment—it's "dogged as does it," thinks he. But the cruel pressure of that ten feet of glued-up bamboo rind presently begins to tell its tale, and the tremulous vibrations of the little rod reveal this fact. For fully the quarter of an hour this struggle goes on, and then the fish gives in, unconditionally, rolls to the surface, and is scooped out—a good three-pounder. But the fight was a poor one, when compared with that made by his neighbour whom he joins in the basket. We wander on, and pick up a fish here and there, returning most of them, as being below our standard, and then go mooning about, bird's nesting, insect hunting, and generally wasting time that ought to be devoted to the catching of trout. But the angler-naturalist—be he ever so keen a fisherman—has eyes and ears for all that goes on around him, and the man who knows most of minute natural history invariably catches most fish. An hour spent in examining the insect life amongst the river weeds, or in a tributary ditch, will yield a rich reward to the student; for it is only by such study that he can expect to understand the why and the wherefore of scientific fly-fishing. To the "chuck-and-chance-it" school of anglers Dame Nature and her secrets are a sealed book; but to the modern fly-fisherman there is far more in his art than the mere slaughter of trout. This is a digression, so we will move on, touching only, with a flying finger, the wren's nest that we peered into, finding the little lady at home, and the colonies of immature sedge, alder, silverhorns, and caperers whom we interviewed in their caddie houses in a shallow piece of backwater.

That colony of caddis, in the water at our feet, would enable us to beguile half an hour away, if you were disposed to join me in the attempt to investigate what varieties of "phregania" are included amongst those "crawling bits of stick" as you call them. They are all flies in the larval state, but inasmuch as there are some two hundred varieties of this one species of case-breeding water flies they afford materials for the study of a life time.

Some people say that the best of all companions in a country ramble is a dog, but he is very much in the way on a May fly-fishing trip. A grand old field spaniel from an adjacent farmhouse took it into his clever old head that he could be useful to us, and being old acquaintances, he came down to the river uninvited and set to work at once. Hunting the water-rats, sometimes in the river, and at others on the bank, he nearly drove us wild, and the look of reproachful sadness with which he met our attempts to drive him home were very comical. Go back he would not; he laid himself down at our feet, with his head on his forepaws, and looked beseechingly at us out of his lovely great brown eyes. There was nothing for it but to take the dog home, so away we went to the house. We foregathered with the farmer, who had lost all his fruit by the frost, and sympathised with him in his trouble; then we set ourselves seriously to the task of making up the number of trout to complete the limit of five brace. It was not a difficult matter, for there were plenty of them, and it was only a question of size. The sun was dropping behind the hill, in the golden west, and the lengthening shadows from overhanging trees put the river in shade; but the rise of May-fly was nearly over. We completed our number of fish, and made our way back to the nearest station with as handsome a basket of trout as any honest angler could desire, tired, contented, and at peace with all mankind.

The long drought has shrunk our little Kentish river Darenth, to its lowest summer level, and the trout fishermen have fared very badly for some weeks past. There are still a few scattered May-fly about—Yellow Sally's, and Undertakers—but the trout have not taken them for the past two or three weeks. As a matter of fact, the May-fly has this season been an utter fraud—the trout cared little or nothing for these tempting insects. Instead of getting baskets of 20lbs. weight, I have had to be content with a couple of brace, on the best lengths of the river—as the result of a long day's fishing. Only one red-letter day, during the May-fly season, has redeemed the miserable failure of this miserable fisherman's carnival. I had fished for eight mortal hours—with only half an hour's break for lunch—and I had used every pattern of May-fly known to the craft. It was blazing hot; there was a sky of copper and a river of brass; and not a breath of air ruffled the glassy surface of the stream. This was the fourteenth consecutive day's May-fly fishing and there was but one miserable three-quarter pounder in the bag, as the result of eight hours' incessant casting. Mentally discussing the matter, I called myself an ass, a monomaniac, and a few other polite things for wasting all these days, and working so hard, by the river side to such small purpose. Finally, I came to the conclusion that fly-fishing was a harmless form of insanity, and that I was really to be pitied, and ought not to be blamed, for my folly. And then I sat me down, in the grateful shade of a grand old tree, and went to sleep. To wake up refreshed, and find the sun dipping the range of

Knockholt hills, and the trout rising madly, was delightful. Weary and disgusted with the May-fly, I mounted a "governor"—a counterfeit of the small bee—which has always proved, in my hands, a deadly evening fly on the Darenth. And the "governor" well sustained his reputation upon this occasion. Commencing with a trout of a pound, others of better quality followed quickly, and the sport became fast and furious. Finally, at nine o'clock, when I finished up, the score stood at five and a-half brace, with five fish going over 2lbs. each. This grand basket was the more appreciated because it came so unexpectedly. I firmly believe that if I had never used a May-fly this season, I should have killed far more trout than have fallen to my lot. But those three hours of evening fishing make amends for many bad May-fly days, and help to neutralise the otherwise bad reputation of the spring trouting this season.

Summer as come upon us at last, and with a rise in the temperature and the reappearance of the sun, the prospects of the trout fishermen have improved; for, hitherto, the low temperature has held all insect life in check, and the cold nights have killed what few of the beautiful water-flies of the delicate "Ephemera" family that were hatched out during the day. This has rendered trout fishing very unremunerative to those disciples of the art who disdain to use any other lure than an artificial fly, so cunningly wrought in imitation of the natural insect, that when deftly cast up-stream, with a gossamer gut line, the treacherous semblance would deceive the wariest trout that ever chalk-stream produced. In spite of all the adverse circumstances of wind and weather—not forgetting to mention rain—I have patiently plied my craft every week since the season opened; but not until the last Wednesday of May was it possible to say

    Wandering by the streams apart,
    Glad and calm as they:
      Plying still my simple art
    All the live-long day;
      Seeking out the shadiest nooks
    Of the winding Kentish brooks.

> Where the pearly waters sleep
> In their quiet pools so deep;
> Where the greedy trout doth lie,
> Ready for th' ensnaring fly;
> Who so free from weeping sorrow,
> And from care, as I?

That description accurately represents the state of affairs on this particular Wednesday, for the weather was all that heart could desire, the lovely Kentish valley in which I fished was looking its best, and the trout rose continuously for fully six hours, myriads of water-flies rising from the river's bed, bursting their chrysalis cases, and taking flight in the glorious sunshine. If you would like to stroll with me for a short distance, let us start together from this broad shallow, which was, until recently, a mill-tail, but the mill-wheel has disappeared, and left a piece of slack water on the opposite bank to where we stand. Some hawthorn bushes, in full bloom, overhang this quiet little pool, and at least a dozen lusty trout, who make it their home, are sucking in iron-blue duns, as they are lured out of the river's current by the false, fair prospect of smooth water beneath the bushes. Let us see if we can reduce the number of that colony; and in order to do so I must go back a little distance, and wade slowly up in the water. This spot will do; and now, with an underhand cast, the fly falls as lightly as a fleck of thistle down, and is immediately snapped up by a deluded troutlet. He shoots down stream like a flash of lightning, as he feels the hook, and I am grateful to him for his haste, because by this move his companions remain undisturbed. With twenty yards of line out, he bores away for the shelter of a friendly weed-bed, but the pressure of my supple nine-foot lancewood rod wins the unequal battle, and with struggling but enfeebled protests, the fish presently comes wobbling safely to net; he is a nice one, a trifle over a pound, with a bloom upon him like a peach, and with spots as brilliant as rubies. Let us try again: "He's got it!" you exclaim. Yes; and the rascal flings himself out of the water, dances a jig, lashes round, and scares the whole colony; then he bores under the stump of the bushes, and manages to get round a stick, and as the water is too deep to admit of my wading to him, there is nothing for it but to put on some pressure, and either break or take. Bravo! we will now basket the pair of beauties on a soft bed of grass, and move on. Someone else has been less successful than myself at this spot, for, hanging upon a branch of the hawthorn bush, dangles a dead sand martin, suspended by a fine trout-line, which, apparently, an angler could not recover without waders. The bird is a young one, with the artificial fly firmly fixed in his lower mandible; and he has been dead about two days—the victim of some preceding fisherman. As it is useless to attempt to catch fish from the bank in this brilliant sunshine, let us go a little higher up, to a stretch of the river which can be waded; and the prospect of sport is here most inviting, rising fish being on the feed as far as we can see ahead of us. We must, however, change our fly, for here no iron-blues are showing, but there are swarms of small black gnats skimming the surface, and tempting the trout to jump half out of the water to capture them.

Here is a beautiful little imitation of the black gnat, made from badger's hair, the hook being no larger than one of the capital letters in the type you are reading. Why not put two flies on, do you ask? For the reason that one fly casts truer, and floats more naturally than a greater number; and in bright weather and clear water such as this, to be successful you must cast lightly, and present your lure as much like the natural floating, living insect as possible. Now, let us make a start, and—keep well behind me, do, or our sport will be spoiled. That was a slashing rise, and I quickly get the hooked trout down stream, to prevent his disturbing the water. He is about the same size as the others, and matches them very nearly in the basket. But, look! there comes the first May-fly of the season: and, by jove! that was a capital fish which snapped him up in a twinkling. Wonder if Mr Trout will condescend to look at my wee midge, after such a luscious mouthful. Just a foot above his nose I place the inviting morsel in the most insinuating manner;

there is a flash in the water, and a turn of the wrist, followed by a rush down stream which means mischief, though it does none; and again the tiny little hook scores another lusty victim—the best trout of the lot. Passing on, we eventually succeed in bringing the contents of the basket up to four brace. This has taken us two hours, and it is now past noon, so let us go over to yonder fallen tree, and do justice to the frugal lunch which a thoughtful better half has stowed away in that little haversack. How exquisitely beautiful appear the spring tints in this flood of sunlight! Men who profess to entertain something akin to pity, only a shade removed from contempt, for those of us who find delight in angling, know nothing either of the mental and physical recreation which the sport affords, or the great love of nature which it engenders in those whose tastes and opportunities have induced them to peep into the mysteries of Dame Nature's many kingdoms. It is very pleasant to sit here on this old log, sunning ourselves, and feasting on the varied beauties of the landscape; whilst, soothed by a pipe, and the lullaby of the river at our feet, we vie with each other in declaring this to be the most delightful valley out of Paradise.

But I am drifting down with the stream of time. It is the tendency of all anglers to do so; we are a race of men doubly blessed; the memories of the past are cherished, for they are full of green fields, babbling brooks and pleasant reminiscences, which no other sport can yield. An angler, if he be worthy of the name, must be something of a naturalist, and if the mysteries of nature are to him a sealed book, then he is only a mere pot hunter, past whom a thousand and one subjects of minute study and keen pleasure glide unheeded and unseen. In the heat of a midsummer day, when the trout refuse to rise, the angler naturalist can lie down upon the river's bank and in the stream beneath him find an inexhaustible source of study that will absorb him and excite his keenest delight. How many of my thousands of readers for instance have ever studied the habits of a water spider? You see the little creature on the surface, and wonder at her ability to walk about the water, as if it was a sheet of glass. Let us lie down and watch the performances of this little insect. A few seconds of close inspection will enable you to see that the wee spider has a single filament of submerged web attached to her. Presently she gives a frisk of her body; and you see an air bubble caught between her legs, and down she goes, by the aid of the rope; the air bubble glistening like a diamond attached to her. She dives beneath a tiny web the size of a sixpence, attached to some aquatic plant, and there loosing the air bubble, it expands her net, like a small umbrella. Look closer, and you will see that beneath this bell-tent are fastened a clustering ball of eggs, upon the safe keeping of which the fond mother expends all her time, returning only to the surface either to obtain food, in the shape of minute insects, or else to replenish her stock of fresh air. How she catches those bubbles with her legs, and conveys them unbroken to her nest, for the sustenance of herself and her young, and how she occasionally takes down with her a small midge as well, are details worthy of the close study of a minute philosopher, and you will assuredly rise from such a study with the humbled conviction that you have yet much to learn.

But there are trout waiting to be caught, and I have vowed either to go home with six brace, or else never to go home again. There are some fine timber trees away up yonder meadow—chiefly horse chestnuts, overhanging the stream—and these generally shelter a few good fish; but the water is very deep, making it impossible to wade, so I doubt whether we can tempt these "whoppers" to their destruction. At this place, another change of fly, you see, is necessary: because that little crowd of insects flitting to and fro in the shade are grey gnats, and there are a couple of good fish sucking them in whenever they touch the water to deposit their eggs on the surface. All the water-flies lay their eggs in that manner, and the egg, sinking to the river's bed, hatches in due course, producing a minute maggot, which, when fully fed, spins about itself a shell-like cocoon, in which it develops into a perfect fly, and only waits until a fitting state of the atmosphere causes it to rise to the surface of the water, break its skin, and take flight. Poking about under trees is not much adapted to our style of dry fly-fishing, but these fellows here are worth trying for, and—by George! I've got him! He's a good one, you can see, by the manner in which he bores low down in the deep water, and refuses to show himself; but the strain upon him will soon tell its tale, although his efforts to rub the hook out against a stone, in spite of the severe pressure of a rod well-nigh bent double, shows he is one of the right sort. Without a wink of warning, he shoots down stream like an arrow from a bow, and when we again come within fighting distance of each other he is entangled in an ugly bunch of brambles, thrown into the river when hedge-trimming went on. I can see the plucky fellow in the clear water, tugging backwards like a dog, turning somersaults like a street arab, and doing his level best to break away, but the bushes yielding, prevent the smash which he is trying to bring about. I try to get the net under him, but the attempt is hopeless, and finally the thorns catch the meshes, and there is work for more than one pair of available hands, especially as the wretched net will not come free. But, why prolong the agony of that inevitable end, which you, fair reader, can foresee? It came at last, and I—no, you are mistaken; I said nothing of the sort. I merely rigged up a new fly, went back to the tree, and killed a fish in very little more time than it has taken to recount this episode—then I felt better. The sun has been gone some time, but the air is balmy. I have been wading some four or five hours, altogether, and have got the requisite number of fish to enable me to return and say triumphantly, "There they are! I told you I should get 'em." And I therefore decline to yield to the keeper's suggestion to fish on. My cry is "enough"; my basket is heavy; there is a good tramp before me; I am hungry as a fisherman, and thirsty as a fish; so, away by a short cut through the meadows, wet with dew, and the air richly laden with the perfume of the hawthorn, I presently repair the wasted tissues at a snug little hostelry, and catch the last train home to Bromley.

THE DARENTH AT EYNSFORD—SPRATT'S POOL.

It is satisfactory to find that the trout have recovered their appetites, after the May-fly gorge, and what splendid fighting trim they are in, as the result of their late high feeding ! Not that the hatch of "ephemera vulgata" was at all a heavy one, or at all equal to those we can remember in years gone by, but there was enough to put the big fish into good condition. The long drought has reduced our sparkling merry little river to so low an ebb that the trout are as shy as trout can be, and it is lost labour to try for them in the shallows ; they are off like scared sheep the moment a line goes over them, no matter how deftly you cast. The day is dull and cloudy the wind has chopped round to the south after a long spell in the north-east ; which has sorely tried the proverbial patience of the disciples of the gentle craft, and sent them home with light creels for weeks past. To-day, however, things look better, there are a good few flies upon the water, and occasional rises of fat blue-winged duns—favourite morsels those—make the big trout jump and souse about in a manner quite refreshing, after their long sulk and steadfast refusal to be tempted to the surface. If the rain will only hold off we may possibly score as good a record as we got upon the same date last year—in a steady downpour of rain which lasted the live-long day. But horror of horrors ! I cannot find any blue duns in my fly-box, and the more I hunt fruitlessly, the more miserable I become from the inward conviction that the only flies these trout will take to-day have been lost out of my box ! Let us, at any rate, do our level best, and it may be that these olive duns will serve as a make-shift because they match the body colour of these luscious "ephemera" upon the water, and we may make up by industry for the imperfections in our lure—it is your lazy fishermen who fail to catch trout, and always rail against their luck. There are a couple of fine fellows under that bough sucking in the duns with a zest which shows that they will not care much about the colour of the wings and here goes my little olive a foot in front of the speckled beauty's nose. She has got it in an instant, and is racing down stream in a manner which admits of no denial, tug-

ging vigorously, although ineffectually, to reach a
friendly weed bed, but her head yields to the rod pressure,
and with open mouth she wriggles helplessly into the net—
a beauty of nearly a pound, and as "handsome as paint."
Her mate is still making big rings undisturbed and inno-
cent of the tragedy which has just been enacted so close at
hand, so we'll just get the fly nicely dried by a few artistic
flourishes, and present it for his acceptance. He's snapped
it ! yes, and flings himself out of water jumping up and
down in a manner which shows that he is lightly hooked
and he'll soon be off—by jove ! he's gone ! Whenever
a trout dances in that way you may be sure he is only
caught by the slightest of holds, and the fish usually gets
rid of the hook by a series of jumps. Those blue duns now
increase upon the water, and my olives are no longer looked
at, a dozen rising fish cast over carefully and unsuccess-
fully, and then we try in despair red gnats, yellow duns, and
everything else that is at all likely to pass muster. This
is dreadfully vexing and tantalising, for with the right fly
there is no reason why ten brace of fish should not be captured, and we will waste no more time, but make for the
village, and hunt up those local " quid nuncs," the parson,
schoolmaster, and tailor who sometimes wield the rod, and
see if they can help us to a blue dun. "He's gone for his
holiday, sir," is the answer at the house of the dominee.
"He's in London, sir," is the result at the parsonage, and
the tailor shows us half-a-dozen dilapidated old flies that
none but a lunatic trout, far gone in brain softening, would
look at, and Mr. Snip candidly confessed that he "catches
most with shrimps !" It is disheartening to have tramped
all this way in waders and heavy brogues, but with patient
resignation we will visit yon snug little hostelry, and order
tea to be ready when the day's work is done, borrow a bit of
sewing silk from the landlady, and see if we cannot manage
to tie some flies to match those upon the water. The
stableyard furnishes the needful blue feather from a pigeon,
and having trudged back to our fishing ground let us
spread a macintosh upon this sloping bank, with the river
at our feet, and here smoke the pipe of peace, whilst I tie a

couple of blues. It's mighty pleasant to sit thus beside the crystal brook, and listen to its lullaby, as bubbling and gurgling over the stones it hurries on to presently lose itself in the mighty ocean. What a world of scientific wonders lie hidden in this stream, and how profound and widespread is the ignorance which makes these wonders a sealed book to the vast majority of mankind! Of the myriads of insect life which people these waters, who amongst our acquaintances can give us the most superficial description, or possesses even the most elementary knowledge? That fresh water mussel shell, for instance, might furnish a theme for an essay upon aquatic boring insects. Those tiny holes which perforate the shell are the work of a minute beetle, no greater than a barley-corn or more formidable in appearance than a lady-bird, yet he has compassed the destruction of the mollusk which tenanted that shell. The subtle and persistent attacks of this little borer were neither unknown or unheeded by the mussel, for deposits of fresh shell-making material over the place attacked, show that the instinct of self-preservation—call it what you please—made him alive to the necessity of guarding against the danger by which he was assailed. But we are going a-fishing and I will not plague you, gentle reader, more than I can help with pryings into the habits and doings of the minute creatures which inhabit the watery world. By the way, that belt of valerien is worth a passing glance, for the drought of the past two years has left it high and dry, and it has thrown out long tender roots above ground, which extend many feet down towards its beloved water ; the source from whence it draws its sustenance and luxuriance. Is it "instinct" which teaches these water-loving plants to throw out their feelers in the right direction? Don't talk to me about the "laws of attraction" ; that is a lame and insufficient attempt to explain one of nature's subtle mysteries. Now then for a trial of my home-made fly, for along this shallow of rippling waters several feeding fish show themselves, and they are less likely to be fastidious than are those shy fellows in the smoother surfaced runs of the river. Yes, I've got him, and he comes down stream as gently as if he knew it was wrong to disturb the water

and thus give warning to his friends of the presence of
an enemy. The blue dun is once more sent flying through
the air, and again another trout falls a victim to the imitation ; two others quickly follow to swell the total slain and
then the threatening clouds carry out their threats, and
proceed to pour out their contents in a steady and business-
like fashion. Insect life disappears from the river's surface, and the swallows no longer skim its waters, but hawk
in mid-air, thus indicating that the flies have mounted
higher in order to avoid being beaten down by the rain,
and are there awaiting the finish of the passing shower.
It is useless to fish in this downpour ; so let us join those
happy schoolboys who are paddling under the arch of
yonder road bridge and catching cray fish. The youngest of
the trio, a big-eyed, curly-headed mother's pet, holds the
spoil ; he is too timid to venture into the water ; and,
having won his confidence by admiring the little fresh
water lobsters which he hugs in an old meat tin, he is
beguiled in his youth and innocence, into telling me all
about himself, his brothers, and his baby sister at home—
who is to have one of the cray fish for herself. "What is
the best way to keep them ?" he asks, with his big eyes
looking at us and reflecting his implicit belief in our knowledge of all such matters and it is sad to tell that the poor
boy, deceived into the belief that the only proper way to
keep a cray fish and bring him up in a respectable manner
was to put him in a canary cage, give him some wet flannel
for a bed, and teach him to whistle. That boy made things
unpleasant at home in the evening, because he was not
allowed to carry out these instructions ; and his clerical
papa expostulated with us subsequently upon the wrong
done by destroying the confidence of youth ! Whether it
was a visitation upon us for our unintentional offence
against the laws of serious sober truth, I know not, but bad
luck attended our fishing for the remainder of the afternoon
until the light began to fade, and then a grand rise of red-
quilled gnat came up from the river's bed, and a capital
hour's fishing made a good ending to the day's trouting.

Whatever may be the feelings awakened in other men by

the sight of stubble fields and corn in "shocks," to the fly-fisherman they bring very sad reminders that his rod and flies will in a few short days have to be laid aside, because the close season upon the Darenth commences with the opening day of partridge shooting.

Saturday's trout fishing in the Darenth was a capital wind-up to a bad season, and I had our length of the river to myself. There was a blazing sun and an easterly wind, and these are my favourite conditions. It not only gives you an up-stream wind, but it always produces more insect life from the Darenth than any other state of affairs. What with mooning about after mushrooms and cooking some of them together with a chop, in our hut by the river side, the sun had got sufficiently westward to put the best length of our water in shade from overhanging willows when I began fishing. It was hopeless to attempt to fish this stretch of the river from the bank, so, getting into a pair of long boots, I entered the stream at the extreme end of our beat, and waited to catch some of the natural flies as they came down upon the surface. It is a curious fact that the water bred flies which are common during the early spring months, and disappear during the summer, always put in an appearance again as the autumn advances. Whether these late hatched whirling blue-duns, and dark olives, are the produce of the spring flies, or of those hatched twelve months ago, is a debateable point, but I incline to the latter theory. Some students of minute insect life declare that the members of the "ephemera" family take two years from the dropping of the egg on the water until they rise to the surface, burst their case, and take flight. My own observations lead me to believe that twelve months elapse between the deposit of the egg and the flight of the perfect fly. But to return to our fishing. There were a few fitful rises ahead of us, and a few scattered flies of various kinds came down at intervals. But they varied from big olives to sherry spinners, and the "fisherman's curse"—a midge begotten of east winds and hot suns. When in doubt play a trump, is a golden maxim in whist, and when in doubt put on a red-quill gnat, is equally sound advice, when fishing the

Darenth. Mounting one of these small flies, on the finest of treble-drawn gut (of doubtful strength), we put the tempting morsel in front of an old stager. But he will have none of it, although the fly passed directly over his nose. He is a wary old trout, lying close under the bank, behind a clump of water-valerien; and I have spent hours over that old rascal on many previous occasions. Whilst meditating what to substitute for the red-quill gnat, I see a fly coming down over him, which looks in the distance very much like a small sedge. He snapped it up without a second's hesitation, and thereupon I changed my lure to a golden-tinselled bodied fly, with a red hackle and sedge wings. Dropping this tempting morsel a foot above his stronghold, the eddy carried it round; there was a dimple, a turn of the wrist, and in a twinkling the hooked fish was dashing up stream, fighting for life. Holding him all I dare, to prevent him disturbing the water above, he stopped short, flung himself out of the water, and returned, with a wild rush to his old quarters. But the automatic self-winding reel gave him no breathing time, and the cruel pressure of the rod compelled him to abandon his haven of rest. Down stream he goes, with a dash, passing close to my legs, and I follow as best I can, with my little finger on the trigger of the reel, and the rod bent double. Will that wretched drawn gut—as fine as human hair—stand this strain? is the thought which fills me with fear. But the trout turns and heads up stream, doggedly boring to the bottom and working round in circles, vainly seeking some friendly weed to aid him in the unequal struggle. But he presently rolls to the surface, and in the twinkling of an eye he is scooped out and thrown out on the bank. The spring balance shows him to be a trifle over 2lbs., and having given him a merciful tap on the head, I admire him for a few minutes and then re-enter the river. Wading upwards, a good fish in mid-stream takes a natural fly, and, at the first cast, I am fast in him. After a game fight he comes to net, a beauty of fully 1½lb. To avoid disturbing the water, I proceed to extract the fly in mid-stream. The fish slipped through my fingers, and in falling snapped the drawn gut cast. He was away like a flash of lightning, and I use words which in print are represented thus ————. In all my angling experience I never dropped a fish in this manner before, and after calling myself a few names, I repair damages and feel better. In fact I console myself by repeating aloud:—

"He may swim to the north; he may swim to the south,
But that beggar has got my fly in his mouth."

Moving upwards, two feeding trout are approached within casting distance, and I solemnly vow to kill them both, or perish in the attempt! But I was not called upon to fulfil the latter part of this vow, because the first fish took the fly boldly, and, refusing to give him sufficient line to enable him to alarm his friend, I got the hooked trout down stream, killed him with a short shift and little ceremony. The third fish shared the same fate, and, wading to the bank, I cried, "Hold enough." Thus ended my season on the Darenth, and he would, indeed, be a greedy angler who was not well content with three such fish as those which graced my creel.

Taken altogether, the season has not been such a bad one as might be supposed, having regard to the drought; but as I fish persistently, my record of two hundred and twenty trout can scarcely be considered other than exceptional. Those anglers who have only been enabled to pay two or three visits to the river during this season, and who have not been able to pick and choose their days—those are the men who, with sad and elongated countenances, will tell you that there are no fish left in the Darenth, and that the fishing in our valley has gone to the dogs.

There is an unwritten law which prevails in Kent, and which ordains that when partridge shooting begins, fishing ends. It is a very absurd tradition, because Darenth trout are now at their best; albeit they are, at the present time, more like May than September trout, so far as regards condition. The season that closed to-day is the very worst that has been known on the river within the recollection of the oldest anglers, and yet there never was a better stock of trout. But they have been difficult to catch through the long drought, and the absence of fly; and it is doubtful whether the bulk of them will spawn until the turn of the New Year. Whatever may have been the habits of the trout in this river—when the opening day for fishing was fixed for Good Friday, and the closing for August 31st—those conditions have now entirely changed. May 1st ought to be the day for commencing, and September 30th for closing; because the trout caught in the first few weeks have not got a wag in their tails—poor things; whereas a September trout, in the Darenth, is full of fight, and the odds are all in his favour—given gossamer gut and a handy weed bed. But there are no weeds, and there have been none this season; and for one fish that broke the surface of the water with his head, a hundred did so with their tails, shrimping and rooting at the bottom for ground food. The same condition of things has prevailed upon all the South of England chalk streams, and the dry-fly men have, as a consequence, wasted their science and their artistic skill upon the desert air. Many of the weed beds, which should have furnished clouds of "ephemera," have been high and dry throughout the whole season, and there has been a great scarcity of surface food. Even the rise of May-fly was of the lightest as to quantity, and the briefest as to duration, that any of us can remember, it was up and gone in ten days, instead of lasting three weeks. Fly fisherman, like farmers, are credited with a disposition to grumble, but they have shared in common the dire effects of the drought of the past season. It has been a good season for the poachers, the men who habitually resort to the Alexandra, the dusty miller and the silver doctor. These pot hunters have scored amongst the tailing trout, when legitimate fishermen have gone home with empty creels and clear consciences, and I am much afraid that the force of these bad examples have tempted not a few from the paths of virtue. It is no part of my present purpose to discuss the ethics of fly-fishing, but we must not judge too harshly the man who, with an empty creel after a long day's fishing, kills a brace of fish on a small salmon fly.

It is an outrage upon our art of dry-fly angling; but the provocation is undoubtedly great, when the river is alive with tailing fish, and they will look at nothing on the surface, however tempting in pattern and however skilfully presented. There have been times in which my valedictory notes on the closing season have been written with a sense of self-satisfaction, and a consciousness that the depleted river deserved a rest; but no such feelings animate me at the present moment, for the season just closed has been the worst I have known in the past twenty-five years, notwithstanding that the stock of trout in the river was never so great as it is at the present time.

THE MOY AT BALLINA.

If I was asked to recommend the best and cheapest grilse fishing in Ireland, I should unhesitatingly say, "Go to Ballina." And the best time to go is usually in that part of June when the fish are running up, relying upon some trusty correspondent on the spot to wire the magic word, "Come!" The route from London is via Holyhead to North Wall, Dublin, thence across the centre of Ireland, passing through Athlone and Roscommon, and branching off for Ballina at Maurulla Junction. It is as well to give the guard a tip, and tell him your destination, because I have known men carried on to Westport through ignorance of the fact that Ballina is on a branch line. This long journey lies, for the most part, through a very flat and uninteresting—not to say dreary—tract of country, in which bog land predominates. By engaging Frank Hearns beforehand as your boatman, you will find everything plain sailing upon arrival. I sent a friend of mine over there recently, and Frank met him in Ballina station between five and six a.m. when the train arrived. A cup of coffee with the stationmaster, and away Frank Hearns took his man, straight to the boat. The tide served, it was Monday morning, and the gasworks' pool was full of fish, and my friend hooked and played nine grilse before breakfast. The Moy divides the town of Ballina, and the banks are walled in by massive stone walls, and the river is spanned by a handsome bridge of many arches. Between this bridge and the "cutts" above is about the best pool in the river. The reader will see it in our first illustration of the Moy. This pool is within a hundred yards of the centre of the town, and the competition for this much coveted cast is often very keen. Of course, the river below the "cutts" is tidal, and this cast only fishes when the tide

RIVER MOY THE GAS WORKS CAST.

serves. There is a rock, just below the "Queen's Gap," which is another good position when fish are running. The angler, placed on this rock, fishes a very fast, but narrow, channel, in which the ascending fish lie, and it was here that my friend hooked his nine fish before breakfast. But in this pool the angler is never allowed to follow his fish, for fear of disturbing the water, and losing the cast. Directly you move someone occupies your position; such are the rules of the Moy. The fishing belongs to Mr. Little, and he gives free permission to visitors to fish, but the salmon have to be given up at the "cutts," and they can be retained at market price, which is usually 6d. per lb. The river is severely netted, in addition to the row of salmon traps which span the stream, as will be seen in our first picture of this river. But the stock of fish is still very great, thanks to the free passage given from sunset on Saturday until sunrise on Monday. Some of the fish which run up from the sea during this period congregate in the pools, instead of pushing through to the Lough. As it is Monday morning we will drop down stream and see the first haul at the netting place. That row of corks which you see across the river, are fixed to the shore at one side, and held by a boat at the other, and the seine will be hauled as soon as a second net has been got ready in its place. When that is done the boatmen bring their end of the net ashore in a circle, and three men at either end then proceed to haul in the seine. Gradually the crescent of corks narrow, and it is evident that the haul will be a productive one, for salmon break the water in their rushes to and fro seeking in vain for an outlet. The purse comes up at last, and the water is lashed into foam by the 274 imprisoned fish, which are the greatest number thus taken in a single haul during my visit. In the good old times, only a few years ago, it was no uncommon thing to get 500 or 600 salmon at one pull of the net, but, thanks to the excessive greed of riparian proprietors they have now killed the goose which lays the golden egg. The salmon, when lifted out of the nets, are struck on the head with a staff, packed in boxes, and sent off to Dublin and England. The Moy is a very short river, and this is the secret of why its fish have survived the excessive netting and trapping which goes on. In the weekly open time a sufficient number of salmon run through into Lough Conn, to replenish the stock, and provide a good head of fish. But what glorious fishing there would be, alike in the river and loughs above, but for this excessive over-netting! A favourite pool of mine is the "Ash Tree Cast," shown in our second picture, and this is below the nets. Whatever fish you hook here are but just out of the salt water, and you may rely upon meeting foemen worthy of your steel. A little lower down-stream is the "Dock Cast," a narrow channel with a very fast current through it, where a good many fish get off, especially the tender-mouthed grilse. On the opposite side of the river the little Bunree stream empties itself into the Moy, and it is a curious fact that the sea-trout all turn off into this stream out of the Moy. There is a shallow bar of rocks extending across the river from the Bunree side over to the dock, and below this shallow bar is the favourite haunt of sea trout. The "boys" fish from this narrow reef when the water is low enough to make it wadeable. Following their example, I had some capital fun with the sea trout, which ran a good size, as did also the brown trout of the Moy. But these latter were remarkably well educated, and, except in the dusk of the evening, I found them shy even of a floating fly. A blue-winged dark olive dun was one of their favourites, and this pattern the natives called a "wall fly." With regard to Moy salmon flies, the Hearns have produced patterns of their own which have acquired a world-wide reputation. Visitors could not do better than trust to the Hearnes for the right fly of the right size. I had a very awkward experience at the gasworks cast, where I hooked a good-sized fish that bolted for one of the arches of the bridge. I was fishing with a very light 14 feet grilse rod, and it was useless to restrain, or even check, the mad rushes of this wild fish. My boatman was in agonies, but nothing I could say would induce him to drop the boat. That salmon fought his way some distance right through the arch, and then the

RIVER MOY—ASH TREE CAST.

rascal came up stream through the next arch ! Of course, he smashed me, and my comment of "Thank God, he's gone!" received a responsive "Amen" from the boatman. But he was very wrath with me notwithstanding, and said it was just foolishness to be using "a thing like that"— referring to my favourite rod—for such fighting fish as those of the Moy. But we set to work and repaired damages, which were nothing more serious than the loss of a couple of links of gut. Our luck appears to have forsaken us, with the lost fish, and the "Goshawk" has no charm for them. I am a great believer in a bit of tinsel for salmon just out of the sea, and I mount a small silver doctor, in spite of my boatman's misgivings. At the second cast there was a splendid head and tail rise, and then the fun began. Like an arrow from a bow he bolts down stream, and then, turning suddenly, races back, throwing somersaults in the air at every few yards as he makes for the broken water beneath the weir. If you want to try what strength a salmon has in fast water try him under conditions like these, on a 14 feet rod and fine tackle. Round the pool again goes the courageous fish, now "jiggering" his head like a dog shaking a rat, now high in the air, now deep under water, now making short rushes and flying leaps, whilst the cruel bending rod continually goads him to further frenzied efforts to regain his lost liberty " Bear harder on him," says Mike, who does not like my fine tackle and gentle treatment, and I therefore give the "butt" until the trembling vibrations of the rod convey the telephone message that the struggle is nearly over, and, barring accident, victory mine. A few more short rushes and the noble fish rolls over on the surface, and slowly, but surely, yields, inch by inch, to the winding line which draws him to his fate. He makes a final struggle, but it comes too late —the net is beneath him, and, in the twinkling of an eye, this silvery fourteen-pounder finds himself in the boat. I see you casting a wistful glance at the basket, Mike, and you shall keep up the traditional custom of the country by wetting him with a drop of the "crathur." This bit of good sport restores the good temper of my attendant, and we kill a couple more before the tide fails us and the fish go off the feed. Yes, my friends, I wrote those last four words deliberately, for I am as strongly convinced that salmon feed in fresh water—when they can get food—as I am that anglers drink water—when there is nothing else obtainable.

By the way, I may here mention that the charge for boat and man is 7s. 6d. per day, plus the usual luncheon, or an allowance in lieu thereof. There are two hotels in the town—the Imperial and the Moy—and I, from force of habit, prefer the latter. They have a branch establishment on the shore of Loch Conn, and anglers can—without extra charge—locate themselves in either house. This is an immense boon to Moy anglers, who are often condemned to considerable spells of enforced idleness, waiting for the tide to serve. The Moy boatmen do not love Loughs Conn and Cullen, neither do they love the men who there cater for the wants of anglers. But the visitor must not be influenced by these local jealousies, because the lough fishing is really very good, and cross-lining has now been abolished. There is a good deal of trolling done with both spoon and Devon minnow but I preferred to drift and cast over "The Strand," and troll back to windward when we finished our beat. The salmon upon entering Lough Conn all follow the same course, passing over the shallows of "The Strand," where they take a fly. The fishing is here free, and the angler can keep all he catches. Perch are a nuisance to the troller, as they will take a spinning bait half as big as themselves, and thus cause much waste of time and temper. Lough Conn is connected with Cullen by a narrow channel, but whether the local legend—that both loughs flow into each other—is true, I do not pretend to say. The theory of my two boatmen was that Cullen flowed through one side of the channel, and Conn went through on the other side. I got several of the famous gillaroo trout—with thickened stomachs like a fowl's gizzard, and I hurt the feelings of my men by declaring that they were only common brown trout. The thickening of the coats of the stomach is due to the fact of these trout feeding on water snails, in the digestion of which much friction must necessarily occur. We had much argument upon the subject, but I silenced my men by asking "Did you ever see a young gillaroo—say a yearling?" Of course they had not, for the reason that these trout do not take to a snail diet until they attain to a good size. Of the mighty pike which are occasionally caught in these loughs I heard many tall stories, but the biggest was that of a fifty-pounder gaffed by Mike Hearns, who found the monster choking with an eight-pound grilse half way down his throat. Allowing a discount off the weight of the grilse, I see no reason to doubt the rest of the story.

Ordinary loch flies kill trout on both Conn and Cullen, the three favourites being claret and mallard, olive and grouse, and black and mallard, ribbed silver. Greenwell's glory is another good spring fly, but the local patterns appeared to me rather too large except for a rough water. And it can be rough on Lough Conn, as I proved, for we had half a gale of wind, which lashed up big waves that broke over the gunwale of our stiff boat. But the trout were mad on, and the discomfort of wet clothing, standing in the water up to your ankles were minor considerations! And how the big trout fought in that rough water! It was not the pleasantest part of my holiday to this part of Mayo, but it was one of he best bits of lough fishing I ever had the luck to meet with. In order to enjoy lough fishing, the angler should provide himself with a macintosh petticoat; they are easily carried, and there is no other garment equal to them for boat work in bad weather. A short macintosh and sou'-wester should complete the outfit.

LAKE VYRNWY, NORTH WALES.

"Where can I get some really good trout fishing, combined with comfortable quarters and fine scenery, within a few hours' ride from London?" This is a question which you my friends, are no doubt constantly asked, especially at this period of the year. Symptoms of trout fever are beginning to make men restless, and incline them to seek fresh fields and pastures new for the coming season. To all such I say, Go to Lake Vyrnwy, where every one of the above enumerated conditions will be found to exist, and where—no matter wind or weather—real good sport, and plenty of it, can be absolutely relied upon. London anglers do not appear to have realised what a veritable fisherman's El Dorado there lies waiting them, within a reasonable railway journey from Euston Square.

But before going on to describe the sport, let me first say a word or two about the journey, and what the angler will find when he gets there.

To begin with, this magnificent sheet of water occupies a valley five miles long on the southern side of the Berwyn range of mountains, and ten miles south of Bala. This information will enable my readers to fix the locality. There are several ways of getting to the lake from London, but the best is from Euston to Llanfyllin, $205\frac{1}{4}$ miles; but passengers should be careful not to miss changing on to the Cambrian branch at Llanymynech Junction.

As it is a hopeless task for a southerner to attempt the pronunciation of these Welsh names, the safer way is to write them down in a pocket-book. An official at the aforesaid junction is a choleric man, and when I asked if I changed there for Llanfyllin, he slammed the carriage door and shouted "No!" As the train was on the point of starting, a fellow-passenger came to my rescue, and I jumped out in

the nick of time. Then that red-faced and irascible official gave me a lesson in Welsh pronunciation, and vowed that I had never asked for Llanfyllin. Neither had I, as he pronounced it. Intending visitors, note this fact.

There is a lovely drive of twelve miles from Llanfyllin to the lake, and, given fine weather, this portion of the journey will be much appreciated by lovers of the picturesque. Conveyances from the Lake Hotel meet visitors at the station by appointment, and it would not be wise to risk the chance of getting a vehicle at Llanfyllin, as it is a very quaint little one-horse place, although it is a chartered municipal borough. The drive, as I have said, is a very pretty one, and, as the end of the journey is approached, there are some awkward places in the road that you would not care to drive through on a dark night. Dipping down into the valley of the river Vyrnwy, a merry stream, about equal to the Dove, in the Dale, the expectant angler finds himself in close proximity to the lake, but fails to get a view of it until the height, on which stands the hotel, is reached, and then you see stretched out before you the panoramic view of this beautiful sheet of water.

You, my angling friends, care little or nothing about who made the lake, or how it was made: it is a thing of beauty, and it will, let us hope, remain to the lovers of fly-fishing a joy for ever. It fills a lovely valley, five miles long, with mountains rising from the water's edge; and no one would imagine, to look at it, that this beautiful expanse of water was artificially constructed. But such is the case; and how it was done, why it was done, and who did it, can all be found in the records of the Corporation of Liverpool. We fishermen are not interested in the details. What we want—having arrived at our destination, and feasted our eyes upon the glorious panorama of Vyrnwy valley—is to make the acquaintance of the enterprising sportswoman who has the pluck to develop the angling resources of this fisherman's Eden, and then to test what she has done for the creature comforts of those who pay Lake Vyrnwy a visit. Trust me, brother anglers, you will not be disappointed; and do not be disconcerted either by the luxurious appearance of the hotel, or the admirably-served meal with which you will be regaled. The lessee of this establishment—who also holds the sporting rights over the whole of the mountains which form the water-shed of Lake Vyrnwy —is one of the best hostesses in the United Kingdom and those who visit here are treated upon those generous terms which are calculated to induce you to come again. The hotel is, in truth, replete with all the comforts of a well-ordered house, and a man who comes here on fishing bent, can be taken in and done for at an inclusive charge of three and a-half guineas per week. Of this comfortable hostelry some grateful anglers have written, with poetic fervour:

"We were out for a spin, and we stopped at this inn,
Where there's plenty of grub for inflating the skin.
The fishing was splendid; Miss Davies was good;
Stop if you can; we would if we could."

The lady immortalised in the foregoing verse is the manageress and lessee of the establishment, and a real good one she is, too, as every grateful brother of the rod will testify who visits Lake Vyrnwy Hotel. It is perched on the top of a bold bluff promontory, a thousand feet above sea-level, and from your bedroom windows you command a view of the whole lake. So much for the hostelry; but let me add that it contains all the resources of a good family hotel, including a ladies' drawing-room, and a first-class billiard table.

Now let me briefly describe the lake.

To begin with, this noble sheet of water fills a bottle-shaped valley, with the neck end blocked by a mighty dam of solid masonry, which looks like a bridge of many arches, as seen from the lake itself. The hotel is situated at this narrow end, and the distance to the other extremity of the water is five miles. The lake covers an area of eleven hundred acres. At the upper end are three sequestered bays shut in by mountains clothed with pine woods, dwarf oak, and heather. The shores are covered with verdure, and ferns abound everywhere in great profusion. In one or other of these deep indentations from the main lake you can always find plenty of sheltered fishing water when the lake itself is lashed into fury by a raging gale, and no boat could live on it. I had one such day last July, in the bay shown in the illustration, when the trout rose furiously over the whole of the water, and not one of the seventeen which came on board was much below a pound. They scored 15lb., as the hotel log-book will bear witness. There is at all times good fishing in these bays, but they are, as I have already explained, five miles away from your base, and there is equally good fishing close at home. As a matter of fact, there are trout to be caught around the whole of the twelve (or is it fourteen?) miles which form the margin of this lake; and some of the best I took were taken along the bank near the tower. But the trout rove, and you are just as likely to strike a shoal in mid-lake as around the margin.

I ought, before going farther, to explain that the lake is encircled by a good level road, cut out of the mountain-side, and those who prefer shore fishing can enjoy it to their heart's content. The most successful method is to take a boat, and coast round the margin of the lake, casting in to the bank, and working your flies outwards. It is not often that you get taken more than six feet from the bank in this method of fishing deep water; but in the bays above referred to the whole of the water should be fished over in the usual style of lake fishing, because the bottom can be there touched with an oar.

What grand fighting fish the Loch Levens are! My little ten-foot split cane rod—on which I have killed many 3lb. chalk-stream trout in the May-fly season—was no better than a child's toy against a pound Loch Leven in Lake Vyrnwy. I had to mount a substantial twelve-footer, and even then some of the fish took as long to kill as a fresh-run sea-trout.

To enable intending visitors to identify by name the various portions of the lake, let me briefly enumerate them. To start from the boathouse, two hundred yards from the hotel, the visitor will there find a fleet of some fifteen stiff-built, sea-going craft, moored snugly in Cynon Bay (fed by two streams); and passing out of the stone arch, which shelters it from the westerly gales, we will skirt the northern shore. The picturesque tower, which is used for filtering purposes, generally shelters a good fish or two about its walls, waiting for flies to drop therefrom—a word to the wise. Thence we reach Cedig Bay, a pretty indentation, into which flows a mountain rivulet, which is of considerable volume in times of heavy rainfall. Still hugging the shore, we reach the bay shown in our illustration—Rhiwargor Bay—this has a good-sized river running in at its head. This bay is shut in by bold mountains, rising abruptly from the water's edge, and it is altogether about as delightful a spot as an angler could wish to find himself in. Passing round, we find ourselves in Eunant Bay, with a river flowing in at its head, and a little island around which good sport is often got. The upper end of this bay is now commonly called the Mayor's Parlour, but I fancy the name has recently been given in honour of the late Mayor of Liverpool, who here made record scores. Passing hence, we turn our faces down the lake, and presently reach the indentation of Llwyn Rhiw Bay.

Along this shore are several mountain rivulets, and one delightful waterfall, which you reach by pushing your boat beneath a big stone bridge. Look up at the roof of the arch as you go through, and you will find it hung with white stylactites of considerable length. The waterfall descends from a considerable height, and if you get out of your boat and stand on a rock at the left-hand corner of the arch, you can command the whole pool, and ought not to leave it without a brace of good ones. That you will be charmed with the sylvan beauty of this nook, goes without saying, provided you have any appreciation for what is beautiful in Nature. There are a few more nooks—which I need not describe—on the way down to the dam, and it will pay to cast into the stones of this structure, for good trout often lie there. Thus we reach the shore in front of the hotel—which is as good fishing as any part of the lake—and pass into the boathouse bay from whence we started.

There are two kinds of trout in the lake—the aboriginal brownies, and the four hundred thousand Loch Levens put in some four years ago, which have thriven amazingly, several in excess of 2lb. having already been taken. There are some monster trout in the lake, and I saw a magnificent rise of these big fellows, one Sunday evening, when the water was like a sheet of plate glass, and if there were not fish amongst them ranging from 4lb. to 8lb. then I am no fisherman, and don't know a trout when I see one. These big fellows were rising in mid-lake, with 70ft. of water under them, and there was not a breath of air out of the heavens to ruffle the glassy surface of the water. It is always thus; man never is but always to be blest, and there never was, during my stay, such another calm evening and mad rise as occurred on that blessed Sabbath eve. These big fish never have been tried for by a dry fly man, who understands the science, but there is a big record waiting for the lucky fellow who happens to catch them in tune. It is true that men homeward bound in the gloaming have trailed their flies behind their boats, and been smashed before they realised what they had got on; it is equally true that one man when trailing had his rod dragged bodily out of the boat, by one of these "big 'uns," and never recovered it! My own idea is that the proper way to fish for them is with a dry fly, in the last hour of daylight, and there is no better place to try the experiment than in the deep water immediately in front of the hotel. But the locality must depend upon the rise; it is no use to cast a dry fly, and let it float, in the hope of attracting a big trout to the surface. My own impression is that these large trout are the aboriginal inmates of the old natural lake, which existed before the valley was flooded; and as there is a local record of an 8lb. trout, killed by a parson, in the original Vyrnwy, my theory is based upon more than mere speculation. Be that as it may, the big fish are there, and I have seen them rise with a boil like a salmon, sending out rings that circled out to 20ft. wide; showing broad backs that haunted you all night, and made you dream of fights with monsters of the deep. To a man satiated with the slaughter of a May-fly season just ended, baskets ranging from 12lb. to 15lb. weight, were of far less attraction to me than the presence of those great lazy fellows in mid-lake; but the westerly gales raged, and the "beautiful soft rain" came down in blinding torrents, as if the flood-gates of heaven had been lifted, and so my holiday ended with never a chance at those "big 'uns." Well, well, some more lucky dog will, I hope, catch them in time, and tell us how he did it.

It will be gathered from what I have already said about the fighting powers of these Vyrnwy trout, that drawn gut is useless, and as for flies, the ordinary Loch Leven patterns all kill well. But I would strongly advise intending visitors not to trouble themselves about flies because you can get everything you want at the hotel, and have the advantage of first ascertaining what is the killing fly at that moment in favour with the fish. The lessee of the sporting rights pays great attention to this department, because she knows—as all experienced anglers know—that quite as much depends upon having the right fly on, as depends upon the ability of the angler to use it.

I ought, perhaps, here to mention the fact that, this season the limit of ten brace to each rod per day has been taken off, but a man who is not satisfied with a basket of nearly 20lb. in return for a ticket costing, by the week, 3s. 4d. per day, is a pot-hunter and no sportsman.

As I have said elsewhere, the whole of the margins of the lake yield good sport, but the trout are roamers and it by no means follows that because you score heavily in one place —or draw a blank—to-day, you will do the same on the morrow. Fish all the edges carefully and don't skip places which you think unlikely, because these often prove the best ; and all the theories of natural lake fishing are valueless in Vyrnwy—it is a law unto itself. My recollection does not serve me as to the precise number of rivers and mountain waterfalls there are which flow into the lake, but I remember half a dozen at least, and where these enter are spots which well repay the angler's careful attention. On the other hand, they are not the places which you should run after ; fish your bank along honestly and fairly, and take these inlets as you come to them, otherwise you may, like that legendary snarleyow, grasp the shadow and lose the substance. I emphasise this advice, because the fish here are roaming in search of food, and you never know where you may drop across a lot of them, and convert a bad beginning into a "limit" score.

As a truthful chronicler, I am compelled to mention the fact that the lake contains some chub, and it is equally true that they provoke to wrath those anglers in whom the old Adam has not been subdued. I am one of those. In the shallow bays, at the head of the lake, these wretched loggerheads are the most troublesome, and the lessee wages an incessant war against them, and at spawning time plays havoc amongst them with the net. I am not disposed to say that they are an unmitigated evil because I had abundant proof that the Loch Levens feed upon the chub fry. Several trout of a pound, which I caught, disgorged a handful of baby chub when knocked on the head, and it strikes me very forcibly that the phenomenal growth of these Loch Levens is thus explained. Two pounds in two years from imported fry is certainly a remarkable record in artificial trout culture, and this was done in Vyrnwy. The lake teems with pound trout, and although they are not so thick as to be "squeezing each other out on the bank" like Pat's salmon, yet they are plentiful enough to yield a good basket every day to anyone who can fish at all, with a two-pounder, maybe at the head of the score. Yes, it is real good fishing, and I know of no other place where you can get anything like it.

The lessee has expended a large sum of money in constructing a hatchery, and she is therefore able not only to replace every fish that is caught by putting in fresh stock, but will also be able to turn, year by year, many thousands of two-year-olds into the lake. This is as it should be, if high-class sport is to be maintained, and there should be a great future before this undertaking. It affords ample space for twenty men in boats, and as many bank anglers, to fish at one time without in any way interfering with each other's sport, and next to Loch Katrine, Vyrnwy deserves to rank as one of the most beautiful lakes in the United Kingdom.

Although the rivers running into the lake are small, they afford amusement to men who like fishing rapid mountain streams, running over rocky boulders. And there is at the outlet of the lake, too, a pretty length of river, containing some nice trout that are worthy of the visitor's attention. Nor should I omit the fact that the lessee at the hotel owns three thousand acres of rough shooting on the mountians close by, and that rabbits swarm and grouse crow on those mountains, I can testify upon the evidence of my own seeing and hearing. Widgeon and wild duck breed in the bays of the upper end of the lake, and there once were swans: but, thank the saints and a pea rifle, the place which knew them knoweth them no more.

Having said all I intend to say about the fishing, let me add a word or two—which those can skip who know all about it—concerning the history of this lake. It was formed for the purpose of furnishing Liverpool with a water supply and only a few years ago there stood in this valley the village of Llanwddyn, with its church and two chapels, and farm homesteads dotted here and there. Where this peaceful village stood there is now 70 feet of water ; the dead from the churchyard have been carried up to a fresh resting-place on the hillside, and there re-interred. What became of the living inhabitants of the sequestered valley deponent sayeth not. They have disappeared entirely, and, as if by the wand of a magician, this lovely dale has been transformed into an anglers' paradise, and one more has thus been added to our list of inland pleasure resorts. London was first importuned to adopt this scheme of water supply, but the Board of Works was too intent on jobbery— the diluted sewage of the Thames was good enough for them. Liverpool took what London refused, and Vyrnwy yields them twelve millions of gallons per day, at a cost of something over two millions sterling in capital expended.

In looking over the official record of the slain, kept at the hotel, I find that since the season opened, on March 26th, there have been 3,085 trout taken on the lake up to Saturday last, June 27th, and the weight of these fish was 2 647 pounds. But what a moist place is this ! I thought Done-

gal took the cake for rain, but commend me to North
Wales. With the exception of Sunday—which is always
fine, when no angling is allowed—it has been raining and
blowing great guns from the south-west ever since Wednesday in last week, and after seven days of blustering wet
gales there appears no likelihood of fine weather.

In spite of the gales and deluges of rain which marred
this holiday in North Wales, and rendered it almost impossible to keep a boat afloat on Lake Vyrnwy, we made the
following scores :—Friday (half day), 9 trout, 7lbs. 4oz.;
Saturday, 16 trout, 14lbs. 8oz.; Monday, 17 trout, 14lbs.
8oz.; Tuesday (half day), 12 trout, 10lbs. 13oz.; Wednesday (half day), 5 trout, 2lbs. 6oz.: Thursday, 17 trout,
15lbs. 12oz. Should any of my readers be on the lookout
for a lovely spot in which to spend a holiday, either by
themselves or with their wives, I cordially recommend them
to try Lake Vyrnwy.

As a Sunday walk, I went on tramp to the upper end of
the lake. At the head of the valley of the Vyrnwy we
come to the approach of the well-stocked and beautiful
grouse moor, situated upon the south side of the Bala range
of mountains. The shooting tenants, with their guests,
make the Lake Hotel their headquarters when on the warpath, and the road to the moor lies through a deep gorge,
shut in by towering mountains, with terrible Welsh names,
not the worst of them being Hirddu Fawry, Arau Glenllyn,
and Mawddy ! Through this deep defile a charming trout
s ream—the Eurant—rattles merrily over a rocky course,
and eventually expends its force and loses itself in the deep
waters of the big lake. Nothing short of practical experience would enable you to appreciate either its natural
beauties, or the villainous shortcomings of an adjacent
thoroughfare ! But all things have an end, and so
we presently arrive at the "keeper's tree," and thus
realise that the foot of the moor has almost been reached.
There are a good array of culprits displayed upon the
"keeper's tree," but grey-backed crows and ravens preponderate, although a considerable number of the hawk
tribe are included amongst the slain. A comfortable cot-

tage, with kennels and stables attached, are close handy; the keeper, a spare workmanlike man, is here amongst his dogs, a beautiful lot of setters, a cream bitch with lemon ears being the queen of the party. "Yes," he says, in reference to his display of "gallows-birds"; there are a good many of those grey old crows about the mountains, but he does not give them much rest. "Cats used to be awful," he adds, because when the Vyrnwy village was pulled down, and the valley filled with water, the homeless cats were driven to seek refuge in the mountains, and to fall back upon rabbits and grouse for a living. And now we start the scramble upwards to the shooting ground, the steepness of the climb being somewhat aggravated by a bed of loose stones, which form our track. But the distance is not great, and the beautiful views on all hands well repay us for our labour, quite apart from all considerations of sport. Away to the south, spread out like a panorama, lies the lake without a ripple, and reflecting like a mirror the mountains by which it is encircled. We are now amongst the peaks of the Bala range and no more pleasantly placed or more picturesque grouse moor could be desired. There are a capital stock of birds this season, thanks to the grouse not having been severely thinned last year, seven guns on five or six thousand acres of mountain, when driving, being the most severe treatment to which the moor was upon occasions subjected. Away on the western portion of this range there are probably a couple of thousand acres or more of easy-going ground, which, if not quite as level as a billiard table is at any rate just undulating enough to afford pleasant shooting without too much exertion. Driving-butts, eighty yards apart, cover all the ground available for that branch of the sport, which, year by year, appears to be resorted to earlier than heretofore. The birds here, in common with all those bred on sheep-feed moors elsewhere, are said to be so wild that early driving is absolutely necessary; but whether the presence of shepherds and sheep is responsible for such wildness is open to very grave doubt. Be that as it may, the tenants follow the fashion in the matter of early driving.

This moor belongs to the lessee of the sporting rights over the whole of the gathering ground which supplies Lake Vyrnwy, together with the fishing in the lake itself. The moor thus let off forms only a small portion of the shooting ground acquired by the Corporation of Liverpool to furnish their city with a water supply. These grouse mountains are said to yield an average rainfall of fifty-three million gallons of water per day! It is not the place to which you should go grouse shooting without a macintosh!

THE BUSH.

Water, water, everywhere, but not a drop to drink! What a week we have had in Paddy's Land, the land where the sky is bluer, the grass greener, and the rivers longer and wider and deeper and wetter than in any other country in the world. If you "misdoubt"—as my boy Mike would say—about the wetness above referred to come over to the distressful country at this period of the year and judge for yourself. All last week the wind blew half a gale, and bitterly cold it was, too, whilst the rain rolled along before the gale in vapoury waves, which looked like drifting smoke. Oh! it was lovely weather for fly-fishing! Talk about rain, why the very trees and mountains appeared to be raining, and the earth itself poured forth rivulets and exuded water like a wet sponge wherever you set foot. As for the rivers, their contents might have been bottled, and labelled "Dublin Stout," so brown and frothy was the flood which swept down. But there were poor folk who suffered more from these rain storms than did us holiday folk, because the oat harvest is only half finished in Ireland and there is, on the cold wet land, a quantity of oats not yet cut in the north-western parts of the island. Potatoes are a wretchedly poor crop—small as to size, smaller as to yield, and very much diseased. This I can say is true of the district comprised within the counties of Galway, Mayo, Derry, and Antrim, because I have seen them for myself this season, and in the first three named places the scanty crops will not feed the people beyond Christmas. But I came to Ireland for sport, and not to examine into the probabilities of a famine, although I have found more of the latter than of the former, as the results of my exertions hitherto. The oats may spoil and the praties may rot by reason of the rain, and the rivers may run double stout, but

there is one source of consolation to the sportsman in Ireland at this season of the year—the snipe are plentiful and there are also teal to be had, if you are web-footed, or happen to have brought with you a pair of rubber wading stockings. You may speak as contemptuously as you please about "bog trotters," but I shall, after my recent experience, entertain a profound respect for the natives who can traverse these treacherous and trackless wastes, and lead you out safely after a good day's sport. The precise locality in which I have been floundering after snipe is situate midway between the source of the Bush river and Knocknacarry, on the coast. We found fully a hundred brace of birds, and, as a truthful chronicler, I am bound to admit that I did not seriously reduce the number. My companion in arms carried an ancient weapon, which looked to be far more dangerous to himself than to the snipe; but such was not the case—his powder was much straighter than that from Bromley. Snipe are always more difficult to find after moonlight nights than when the nights are dark. This is a hint which should be borne in mind by those who have not much experience with these birds. They feed at night when they can see to do so, and betake themselves to inaccessible places during the daytime. After a dark night, however, you will find them on the feeding-ground next morning, and, being hungry, they usually lie close and give the guns a fair chance. A good stock of home-bred snipe are reported from their favourite haunts in the wilds of Ireland, which is par excellence the snipe-shooter's paradise. Unfortunately, there are very few men who can really do justice to a good day's snipe-shooting, and the common cause of these failures to kill is that they fire too soon. My friend that I shot with rarely missed a bird, and the "law" he gave them was something astonishing. His gun was an old single-barrelled muzzle-loader, nearly six feet long and the way in which he let a snipe that rose at his feet get seventy yards' start before cutting him over was one of the finest performances I ever witnessed. To-day I have been having a turn on the river Bush, for a late-run salmon, and only got a small grilse, but I had a very pleasant outing along the banks of this beautiful river. I never saw Ireland looking fresher and greener than it is now. There is scarcely a leaf that yet bears the tinge of approaching autumn, and the hedge-rows are ablaze with the dense masses of hawthorn berries which bear down the branches, so enormous is the crop.

As for blackberries, there never was such a crop, and my boy Mike opines that he could load all the Channel steamers with blackberries out of Antrim if the London people would only buy them. He has a fine fertile imagination, has Mike, and it seems a pity that so much latent talent should remain undeveloped. The other day I was invited by a very hospitable neighbour to try and capture one of the many leviathan pike which are said to inhabit an ornamental lake of thirty acres which forms part of the beautiful surroundings of his mansion. Mike was in ecstacies; it was the dream of his existence to fish this lake of whose fabulous pikes he had "hear tell" from his infancy. He told me, with an expression of awe upon his face, that he had "hear tell" of a greyhound attempting to swim across this lake, when the animal was seized and swallowed by a monster pike! Then there was the case of the village shoemaker who set a poaching night line in the lake, and when he went to take it away next morning pulled up a monster of the deep that opened its jaws like an alligator, and barked at him like a dog. This so frightened the poor snob that he ran home and slammed the door, declaring that the beast was chasing him. Such were the stories with which Mike beguiled the time as I alternately spun around the shallows and live-baited 'the deeps, getting nothing bigger than ten pounds, until the shadows began to lengthen. Then the fun commenced, for the fish began to feed. Presently Mike got a run and struck his fish, which gave an angry swirl and went down into deep water, pulling savagely. "Holy Mother," says Mike, "'tis a sixty pounder—devil the ounce less and a savage baste entirely. Och! murder! it's tearing the arms off me, he is, entirely!" But at this moment the rod straightened, and Mike's broken hooks came back, minus his live-bait. To attempt to convey any idea of his lamentations would be useless—he moaned and vowed that he had lost the biggest pike in Ireland. After repairing his tackle I threw over the same ground where the big fish had been lost, and at the second cast the invitation was accepted. After a few minutes' play Mike gaffed the pike, a twelve-pounder, and hanging out of his mouth was the missing part of Mike's tackle and also his lost bait—I had caught his so-called "Monster"! Mike collapsed completely and never said another word until we neared home, when he pleadingly asked, "Your honour won't give the boys the laugh of me about the big pike—plaze don't tell 'em, your honour." And I did not, but I feel sure that Mike will tell the story without the sequel when I am gone, and excite the envy of "the boys," by describing how he hooked and lost the monster pike that swallowed the greyhound and chased the shoemaker to his home.

The Bush is one of the most prolific salmon rivers in Ireland, and some idea of its beauty will be gathered from our illustrations. This is a mountain-fed stream, and, unlike most Irish rivers, there is no lough at the head of the river. As a consequence, the water quickly runs down, and equally as a consequence, the salmon crowd together in enormous masses in the pools, where they become dreadfully diseased. I have seen them netted out in such a loathsome state that they had to be buried and made into manure. As the fishing on this charming little fly river is in private hands—and as it changes hands very frequently—the would-be angler should take up his quarters in the village of Bush Mills, and here ascertain on the spot who is the person to apply to. It is a matter of payment, and not of favour; but the terms are very reasonable.

From Portrush to Bush Mills, and thence to the Giant's Causeway, there is an electric tramcar running, and the Bush is, therefore, very easy of access from the Bann. There is a local fly-dresser in the village of Bush Mills, whose name escapes my memory, but he lives two or three doors from the hotel.

I once had some very good sport on this river with the prawn, when the fish would not look at a fly, and when it was labour in vain to cast over them.

The use of prawns as lure for salmon is comparatively new, and most fly fishermen deplore its introduction. Amongst fish resting in pools, and fresh up from the sea, this method of fishing is often very deadly, but salmon are kittle cattle, and there is never any certainty about them. Like women:

> "When they will, they will, you may depend on't;
> When they won't, they won't;
> And there's an end on't!"

As yet, no two men are agreed upon the right way to fish a prawn, and everyone swears by his own method. Anglers are constantly asking advice upon the subject, but those who are best able to supply the information observe a discreet silence. Few men care to confess that they have resorted to pot-hunting methods of angling, and fewer still will plead guilty to having fallen so low in the scale as to tempt "salmo salar" to his fate with a worm! It is no part of my present purpose to discuss the ethics of angling, but when everything else has failed, I have occasionally resorted to a shrimp—not a prawn—and when my sins are counted I can plead as a set-off that I have never caught a salmon on a worm. And this brings me to the practical part of this chapter. According to my experience, red shrimps will kill far better than prawns, and the shrimps are far more easily obtained, besides being one-tenth of the price of the larger crustacea. In fast rivers, the shrimps should be cast, and fished, exactly as you would a salmon fly, working it slowly, and striking to the rise, or "rug," as the case may be. In deep, heavy pools, where the water travels slowly, float fishing may, and with advantage, be adopted—but do not strike until the first run of a few yards is over, and the float has subsequently "bobbed" twice and disappeared. On the Shannon, and other fast rivers, it is the practice to pass the snood of the hook through the head of the prawn or shrimp, bringing the baiting needle

BUSHMILLS—THE FALLS.

From photo by W. Lawrence, Dublin.

out of the tail, and to bind the bait firmly on to the hook with fine red worsted. This method may save trouble, and be economical, but there is nothing else to be said in its favour. Obtain some freshly-boiled red shrimps, put them into a tin box, with double their own bulk of fine table salt, and they will last a month, but if you can get a fresh supply, at short intervals, do so, because the fresher they are the more fish you will kill. They require a lot of soaking before use, and the longer you keep them in water the more pliant and durable they become. Have nothing to do with glycerine as a preservative; prawns and shrimps so treated are a delusion and a snare. Use long-shanked single hooks; and as you value your peace of mind do not be tempted to try the complicated "prawn tackle," sold in the shops. Annealed steel wire is far better than salmon gut for prawn or shrimp fishing, because it sinks the bait, which has a tendency to rise to the surface when worked like a fly. I have given single steel wire a good trial for two seasons, have killed fish up to $22\frac{1}{2}$lbs. on it, and never had an accident. If you want any stronger proof of its excellence, try it for yourself, provided you can get it. The wire I use would "hang a man," if it did not cut his head off in the process, and yet it is equal in thickness to the finest of natural trout gut.

AUTUMN PIKE FISHING.

November and December are favourite months with me for pike fishing—not that I love it much—because at this period the fish take a spinning-bait much more freely than they do later on in the winter. Flooded out of my autumn quarters in Ireland, and driven out of Wales by a series of deluges, there has been nothing for it but to fall back on the lake pike—the rivers have lost themselves for weeks past amongst the fields ! When neither trout nor salmon are to be caught there are many worse forms of sport than spinning, with natural bait, for jack ; especially if you do it artistically with a light twelve-foot rod and a single salmon gut trace, casting in the Thames style. This is a somewhat trying method of fishing to choleric men when done from the bank, because the coils of the slack reel line have a fiendish tendency to attach themselves to every conceivable abomination in the shape of brambles, twigs, and tufts of grass ! The scene of my latest experience of this kind was in Sussex, at the foot of the Southdown Hills. There was a chain of lakes emptying into each other, and forming the source of a little river. The upper and largest of these lakes at one time encircled an ancient and moated castle, of which only a heap of crumbled ruins now remain ; and the moat on the drawbridge side has been filled in. We found the water slightly tinged with a chalky blue—suggestive of lodging-house milk—and the old miller "'lowed it bain't much good going for them greet pikes when the springs be a-running." But the miller's son, " Garge," was not of the same opinion, and he "'lowed that the guv'nor didn't know nawthing 'bout fishin'." "Garge" lent us a hand to catch some roach for bait, and put us amongst a shoal of big ones that bit madly. A score of beauties were got in less than half an hour, but they were too large for spinning, nearly all being over half a pound—as white and silvery as herrings. The biggest were put into a pail for live baiting, and the smaller fish received their quietus for spinning. We tossed for choice, and the fickle jade favouring me, I took the upper lake, knowing it to hold the biggest fish. The lower end, where the water averages from fifteen to twenty feet, was spun over carefully from the bank — there was no boat — without any response, and " Garge " then put a live snap bait of one pound weight on my spare rod, and left it tied to a tree on the bank. A shout from the next lake announced first blood, and directly we got to shallower water a pretty little five-pounder paid the penalty of responding to my invitation. But it was cruel fishing over a belt of tangled briars that straggled out from the water's edge for yards, forming a tangled mass. Long castings were necessary in order to reach the best water, and my attendant finally hit upon the dodge of spreading his macintosh for me to coil the line on. We landed two small fish that were returned, and killed a very game ten-pounder after a splendid fight. The weeds in the shallows proved an awful nuisance, and the bigger fish appeared to lie in the deep open water, on the outer edge of the weed-bed, thirty or forty yards from the bank. Those devotees of the fly-rod who deny that any skill is needed in pike fishing would find themselves mistaken in such a place as this, especially with a stiffish head wind against them. Having put in an hour or more of this long casting, we had a rest, and smoked the pipe of peace, while " Garge " told of legendary pike of enormous size that were said to inhabit this old moat. Whilst thus engaged a big pike made a flying leap out in the deep water at the lower end of the moat, and away we rushed to our spare rod, and the noise of the salmon reel attached to it announced that a fish was on. We only got there just in the nick of time, for nearly all the line was out, 150 yards, and the fish was fighting in mid-lake like a runaway pony with the bit between his teeth. Come back he would not for a long time, and he bored to the bottom, shaking his head savagely, and my little cane spinning-rod, when strained to the utmost, made no more impression on him than it would on a log of timber. Our friend came up from the middle lake to see the fight, and for stubborn, sulky resistance, it was the best that I have ever known a pike to make. The fish was evidently a good one, its policy was one of masterly inactivity—beyond moving now and then a few yards to the right or left, budge he would not. With a steady strain on him—all that the little rod would bear—the "man at the wheel" waited patiently, sending telephonic messages occasionally by tapping the butt. At these signals Mr. P. "jiggered" viciously, but the spinning flight was mounted on eight inches of silver gimp, and unless the big bait had been pouched, the odds were all in favour of the rod. Presently came a fierce rush in the direction of a shallow weed-bed; the line cut the surface of the water in a half-circle, and the cruel salmon winch wound in every inch that could be gained, the rod meanwhile bent double. But the haven of rest is not gained, and the fish comes at express speed to a pent-stock within a few yards of the bank on which we are standing. Whether or not his intention was to come out on the bank and assume the aggressive instead of the defensive is open to doubt; but he never got round that pen-stock. On the contrary, the slack line was pulled in by long sweeping drags and laid coiled upon the bank, and the exhausted fish was gasping on the surface of the water under the point of the rod. It was all over, for a pike, when he "gives you best," caves in ignominiously and unconditionally, and does not "play 'possum" like salmon to get his second breath and commence the fight again. The gaff did its work, the toe of "Garge's" hob-nailed boots did the rest, and then the spring balance recorded 16lb. 4oz. as the weight of the victim—a female fish, heavy in roe. Yes, I know that in the foregoing description of the fight the sex of the fish has been spoken of in the masculine gender, but how was I to know that it was a lady that I had thus been treating so cruelly, until the end came, and we stood face to face? Even now I should not have undeceived you as to the sex of that pike but for the fact that thereby hangs a tale. The roe of that pike weighed $1\frac{3}{4}$lb., and fifty-six of the eggs weighed four grains. As there are 12,250 grains in 1¾lb., it follows that there were no less than 171,500 eggs in this fish! I commend these figures to the consideration of those persons who think that a few pike are not injurious to a trout stream—that they only kill the sickly fish and a few small fry!

It would be but a tame record to tell what we did after the capture of this sixteen-pounder. It is true that we put up for the night at the mill; it is equally true that I left my spinning bait on the flight of hooks, and caught the miller's cat during the night. Equally true is it that we constructed a raft next day, with a field-gate and some "wattles" for a foundation, and all the stray planks and bits of timber we could collect by way of a deck. Equally true is it that we got into mid-lake on this crazy craft, and that in the excitement of gaffing a big fish we upset the concern, and all three of us were shot headlong into twenty feet of water! But these are only trifling incidents connected with our holiday. After all, pike fishing is not to be despised if there is nothing better to be got.

In common with a good many other anglers, I want to catch a leviathan pike, but hitherto the fates have been against me. Twice, at least, I have been very near the realisation of my ambition, but, you will say, those lost fish always are monsters! A man of my acquaintance suffered from the big pike mania to such an extent, that he, being possessed of ample means, devoted his whole time to the search after one of these monsters. And what is more, he captured one at last, and has lived happy ever after. This is how it happened. Two of us made a serious effort to beat the Irish pike record, and the fact of our attempting such a task shows how badly we were bitten by the craze. The loughs of Antrim, Derry, Donegal, Sligo, and Mayo were each and all tried in turn, and great was the slaughter of "Esox lucius," but nothing over 20lbs. did we get. A few grand trout fell to our pike lures, and of these fish a 14lbs. Lough Neagh trout took a 4-inch gold spoon! Well, to get on with this true pike story. We finally laid siege to Lough Derg, of whose mighty pike the oracles of Killaloe are never weary of discoursing in London angling papers. Here I did get hold of a veritable monster, hooking him in thirty feet of water, on a huge spoon ; and after having him on for upwards of an hour, he either weeded me, or else got round a rock, and it took the united efforts of two men to break the tackle. This fish only showed himself once, and he was 4ft. 6in. long if he was an inch. Next day my friend killed a 20lb. pike, spinning a pound perch for a bait; but we were in search of forty pounders, and our man Mike vowed that the lough was just paved with such monsters! He further assured us that when the salmon smolts came down on their way to the sea, these big pike moved in a pack to the neck of the lough, where the Upper Shannon enters, and there congregated in thousands, to feast upon the young samlets. This story we repeated in due course to the man whose life was dedicated to the capture of a mighty pike. Forthwith he equipped himself, as if about to start in search of the North Pole, and off he went to Ireland. We heard of him first from the quaint old town of Neenah, and then he was lost to us for many months, until one day a telegram arrived, saying, "I have got him at last, 35lbs." This grand fish was killed on a large spoon bait, of native manufacture, carved out of a cow's horn! I saw that pike, after it was mounted, and it took me months to recover the attack of envy, hatred, malice, and uncharitableness, which the sight produced. In fact, there has been a coldness between us old cronies ever since. You can forgive a man almost everything else, except beating you at fishing. After all, it was only an Irish pike, and 35lbs. was nothing of a fish for a country whose pike had swallowed greyhounds when swimming in the lough, and who thought nothing of a 10lb. salmon for a meal. At least, that is what several Irish boatmen have assured me; and if they are not to be implicitly relied on, our confidences in such matters are nowhere safe! There was some small consolation to be got out of such disparaging remarks, and we used them, as we set to work again in search of an English thirty pounder. Whilst on this quest, I had one of the very best day's pike-fishing that has ever fallen to my lot. It was in a large Kentish lake, some 18 acres in extent—in midwinter—and the jack were madly on the feed. Everything under about 8lbs. or 10lbs. was put back, and yet we took away a hundredweight, including a 3lb. perch. But the missing monster was not amongst the slain. Only once since that disaster on Loch Derg have I been within an ace of scoring a record pike. It was down in Sussex, and I was spinning a lake, from a little cockle-shell of a punt, poling her about the shallows with my landing-net handle, there being no oars in the boat. After making a long cast, and commencing to slowly draw in line, my bait—a big roach—stopped. "Bother those weeds," I exclaimed, and giving a savage tug, it was responded to by the terrific rush of a hooked fish. He took about seventy or eighty yards of line off the reel, and then settled down like a log on the bottom. Fight he would not, stubborn, passive resistance was his policy, and as he was in 15ft. of water, he kept well down out of sight, boring on the bottom. My friend on the bank shouted to remind me that he had got the gaff, and that I was too far out to pole the boat! The situation was serious, but the first thing to do was to kill that fish; and to do this I tried my utmost. After boring about like a submerged torpedo for half an hour, the great pike rolled to the surface, and I saw at length the ambition of my life was gratified—it was a veritable monster of a pike. But lift him in the net I could not; for it was not deep enough, and twice he slipped out and renewed the fight. Finally, by the advice of my frantic friend on the bank, I agreed to run the fish, head foremost, into the net, and try him that way. Woe is me, he slipped out, the spinning flight hung in the meshes of the net, the fish struggled, tore out the hooks, and then he sank in deep water. That he was a veritable thirty-pounder, I am prepared to make solemn affidavit; and it is borne in upon me that this was my last chance of securing a record pike.

Hope springs eternal in the breast of the fisherman, and so it happens that we never abandon ourselves to blank despair, but keep trying again. A glance through some of the authentic records of big pike, that have fallen victims to the angler's skill, is enough to encourage anyone to hope on. The Irish largest pike of which there is any reliable account is mentioned in Buckland's "Curiosities of Natural History." This fish was found dead by Martin, the water-bailiff on Lough Corrib, and it measured (the pike, not the lough) 5ft. 8in. long, and would, consequently, weigh from 100lb. to 112lb., according to the approved methods of arriving at weight for length. The famous 72lb. pike taken in Lough Ken, co. Galway, was measured by the Rev. W. Houghton (and attested by the Hon. Mrs. Gordon), who gave the length as 7ft., and breadth of skull, 9in.— a veritable fresh-water shark. Within the past ten years only one English pike has been captured that has been proved to exceed 50lb., and Norfolk contributed this specimen. Coventry yielded a 35lb. male pike in 1890, and the River Lea furnished a twenty-seven pounder in 1891. The largest English pike of which there is any thoroughly trustworthy record was captured in Whittlesea mere, and weighed 53lb. The champion pike fisherman of the present generation is Mr. Alfred Jardine, and the top weights amongst his exhibits of pike at the "Fisheries" were one of 36lb., two of 30½lb. each, and several others over 20lb. apiece. These were all English specimens, and the largest was taken at Leeds Castle in 1877. He has since raised this record with a 37lb. pike from private waters in the home counties, and his score amongst big pike will take a lot of beating. December is the best month of the year for pike fishing, as the fish are then in splendid condition and good fighting trim. Later on they become too far advanced towards spawning, and they then show but poor sport to the angler.

Fly-fishermen, as a rule, profess a great contempt for "Esox lucius," but "hungry dogs eat dirty pudding," and when salmon and trout are out of season there are many worse forms of sport than spinning for pike. He would be a difficult man to please who was not content with a day

THE AVON BELOW SALISBURY.

or two on the Avon—anywhere between Salisbury and Christchurch—and he would, moreover, belong to the noble army of "duffers" if he failed to kill a good basket of pike. The Avon is very similar in character to the Itchen and other South of England chalk streams, and it flows through a richly wooded and fertile valley. The river itself and all its surroundings appeal strongly to the instincts of the angler, and tempt him to say, "I could put in a week or two here, even if I did not catch a fish." My last Christmas eve was spent in a punt on a private length of the Avon, and it was one of the coldest day's fishing that ever fell to my lot. There were two of us besides the keeper (who did the punting), and we had a merry time of it. The air was bright, and crisp, and the north wind cut like a razor. Our chief difficulty was to get the line through the rod rings, because they filled with ice as fast as you cleared them! The water was as clear as crystal, and somewhat low as a consequence, and the pike took a spinning bait badly. We had a lot of live roach and dace—big fellows—that were taken out of the Avon in a cast net. A spot was ground-baited, and a pailful of quarter-pounders were caught at the first throw of the net. Up to lunch time we had taken nothing larger than 4lb. or 5lb. apiece, and we then drew the punt into the shelter of a reed bed, where a small bay had been formed by a small tributary stream. The water was here some ten or twelve feet deep, and it eddied gently round, forming a quiet resting-place for a large fish. The keeper declared that it always held one or two of the biggest pike in the river, and we accordingly put out live bait as we discussed cold fowl, and afterwards smoked the pipe of peace. The keeper did not want to move, although we had searched every inch of the water over and over again. We began to get irritable, and even suggested that he disliked handling his ice-coated punt-pole. Still, he did not move the boat, and my companion, winding-up in disgust, dropped his bait close alongside. There was a flash from amidst some rotten reeds, and we both saw a big pike rush off with the bait in his mouth. My friend struck hard, and the fish tore away down stream at a racing pace, in a manner that brooked no denial; but he considerately pulled up before there was any need to follow. Come back he would not; in fact, he had no desire or intention to discuss the matter at close quarters. But fate and the tackle proved too strong for him at the end, and when he eventually received his quietus, and was found to scale 15lb., we unanimously declared he was a beauty. The Avon pike are all long and slender fish, and that fifteen-pounder looked quite 20lb. when seen in the water. He was the best fish of the day on our length of the river, but a friend who was fishing below us killed an equally good one that same afternoon. In very severe weather live-baiting succeeds much better than spinning on this river; but some of the riparian proprietors object to the use of live bait. It seems a great shame, however, that such a grand trout and grayling stream should be sacrificed by the preservation of pike. But the river is in private hands along the length herein referred to, and combined action amongst the owners appears to be impossible. Whilst we deplore the desecration of so charming a water, by leaving it to swarm with the "water wolf," we would not wish to fish for him amidst more delightful surroundings. Perhaps a trifle less than fifteen degrees of frost would be an improvement upon our last Christmas eve experiences, but that is quite a matter of taste.

THE USK, ABERGAVENNY.

THE USK.

Of all the sports which Englishmen engage in there are none so uncertain in their results as the pursuit of the lordly salmon. The only thing of which you may be perfectly assured, in this connection, is that the cost will be far and away beyond all proportion to the sport obtained. Salmon fishing is a pure lottery, even on the best of our rivers, and it is the chance of drawing a prize—in the shape of a few real red-letter days—which lures so many of us to ignore past failures and to try again. What the season will be, when the end is reached a few weeks hence, none of us can foretell. Given a wet autumn, the "back-end" may yet make amends, to some extent, for the spring and summer fishing, which have, to put it mildly, been rascally bad. As an illustration of the glorious uncertainty of this costly sport let me instance the Monmouthshire Usk. Last season the rod-fishermen killed on this splendid fly-river no less than five thousand salmon! With such a magnificent "record" score to point to, the fancy rents which there prevail went up with a bound, but those who paid them in haste have had the whole of the present season wherein to repent at leisure, for, up to September 1, it is doubtful if twenty "fish" had been killed by rod and line on this river. Hope springs eternal in the breast of the fisherman, and he never is but always to be blest; therefore we found in the lovely valley of the Usk, at short intervals, men clothed in strange fishermen's garments and weary woe-begone countenances, aimlessly wasting their days, and fervently praying for deluges of rain which would not come! Within the memory of that historical and respected individual, the oldest inhabitant—who never remembers anything—the river Usk has not been so low as it has been this season. So low, indeed, had it fallen that, in the vicinity of Abergavenny, you might cross some of its shallows wearing a pair of shooting-boots without getting wet-footed, whilst the water in the upper reaches was reduced to the proportions of a brook! The whole of South Wales and Monmouthshire have this summer been phenomenally dry, and the only chance that remained to those anglers who have paid big rents was the chance of the river getting up several feet above its present summer level. Nothing short of seven days' downpour could save the salmon anglers on this river from a blank season, but given those watery conditions, and the fish would come racing up in their thousands like a pack of hounds!

I had got thus far in my account of the hard fate of the Usk anglers when the floodgates of heaven were opened, and its long pent-up waters descended upon South Wales, to the great joy of the patient and long-suffering salmon anglers. On the first of the present month (September) the upper reaches of the Usk fished, for the first time in this season, and seven clean salmon, with sea-lice on them, were taken. Two of these fell to my rod, and were taken on Dan O'Fee's silver-bodied "judge," a very killing pattern for fresh run fish. The local anglers in the Usk valley are wedded to a large and coarse dressing of "Jock Scott," and scarcely use any other fly if there is the slightest tinge in the colour of the water.

Now that fish are to be caught on the Usk, perhaps I may supply some useful information by saying that there is no difficulty about getting a day or two on this river. By making Abergavenny his headquarters the would-be salmon angler can get his choice of two or three pieces of water, for which daily tickets are issued at a reasonable price. On one of these lengths of the river I saw three nice fish killed last Saturday; and to men whose means and time are limited, and whose love of fly-fishing is great, these waters now offer the certainty of sport. When I say "certainty," let it be understood that this mountain-fed river will jump up three feet in an hour with rain in the mountains, and that it becomes a raging torrent, like unto tomato soup, both in colour and consistency, upon the slightest provocation.

There is a good length of the river, close to the town, rented by an association, and day tickets at 5s. can be had by visitors. Mr. Pritchard, the principal hotel proprietor, is also the tenant of several lengths of good fishing, and the wandering angler will find him a useful man to consult.

We were very unfortunate in our Usk speculation, because we took a length of the river for a month, and found, afterwards that the man who let it did not possess the exclusive right of fishing! As a matter of fact, there were two anglers wading in our best pools, when we first started to fish.

Deep wading is necessary in many parts of this fast river, and as the bed of the stream consists, for the most part, of red sandstone, it is very dangerous. In some places the water flows over these shelves of stone, not deeper than a foot or two, and then drops into a hole ten or fifteen feet deep. With a spate on it is very unsafe for anyone unacquainted with the river to wade it. When the flood last week began to subside, an owner of an upper reach of the river very kindly invited me to come up and fish it. The river there became fishable two days before it was fit at Abergavenny, there being a lot of discolouring matter discharged from a little stream at Llangriney. We had a most delightful drive through this lovely valley of the Usk, and were charmed with the sylvan beauty of the river as it flowed through a rocky gorge above Crickhowel. There is, by the way, a pool in this village, which visitors at the principal inn can fish. But this is a very dangerous spot and some anglers' lives have here been lost when wading. We found the water on our beat somewhat high in colour, but it could not be fished without wading, as the "catch" laid along under the opposite bank, and the river was fringed on both side with overhanging trees. My attendant said he knew every stone in the river, and he averred that there was only one dangerous spot, just opposite a bush, which he pointed out. Finally, it was arranged that he should watch me from the bank, and give me warning if I approached danger. The stream was very strong, but not more than three feet deep, and the salmon were lying in easier water, close in to the side. At the end of the first fifty yards a big boulder jutted out, from behind this came a spanking rise, and I was fast in an Usk salmon. It is not easy to get ashore under such conditions, with a fighting fish and a heavy press of rushing water to contend with. But I managed to get on dry land eventually, and the fish came to gaff without mishap—a pretty little clean salmon of seven or eight pounds. Before resuming operations, we again discussed the locality of that dangerous shelf of rock, and my attendant was emphatic in his statement that it was immediately opposite the bush. Fishing the water carefully down to within about thirty feet of the bush, I went one step further, and stepped into space! In an instant I was in a hole fifteen feet deep, and being swept down by the rushing waters. Fortunately I can swim like a duck—thanks to my sailor experiences—and I never lost my head for a moment. Holding my rod in the left hand, I struck out strongly for the shore, and soon touched bottom some fifty or sixty yards lower down. My attendant was busily engaged in a vain attempt to light his pipe, and had not seen what had happened to me. What I said to him is immaterial, but it was something very plain and very emphatic. He quietly remarked, "Well, you are only a bit wet; but a parson was drowned in that hole not long ago"! I have heard men say that it is unsafe to strap your waders round your chest, and that it is much better to have your waders full of water than to have them inflated like a balloon. After this experience I believe in the strap. I also believe that I should have shared the fate of that parson had my long waders filled with water.

Wringing out my wet garments, I put them on again, and returned to the fishing. The fly was taken almost immediately, and a second salmon was quickly added to our score—a better one this time. We went back to the head of our length of water, and foregathered with two men fishing above us. They had five salmon between them, running from 5lb. to 16lb. apiece. I did not quite equalise their score before the day was out, but I only fell one short, and but for my ducking believe I should have beaten them.

There are some anglers who affect to despise autumn salmon fishing, but I am not of those, because a fresh-run fish—clean from the sea—is by no means to be despised, even in the month of October. There is, of course, a very wide distinction to be drawn between a "potted" fish, that has been in a pool of the river many weeks, and there grown as red as a copper kettle, and a salmon that has remained in salt water until the autumn floods induced him to run up the river. I grant you that even these bright fish fight more heavily, and that they lack some of the fire and fury of the spring runners; but I am not disposed to admit that these late runners are unworthy of our steel. On the contrary, any experienced anglers will be able to recall many magnificent fights they have had with late fish. Go spring-fishing for salmon, by all means, if you can get it, but should the fish be kept back in the sea, as they have been in many places this season, there are compensations to be found amongst the autumn runners. But I have wandered somewhat wide of my text, which was the glorious uncertainty of salmon-fishing. Returning to this branch of our subject, let me say in conclusion that the man who rents a length of river for the catching of the king of fishes, needs the purse of a Rothschild, the contented spirit of a Diogenes, and the irrepressible cheerfulness of a Mark Tapley.

KILLALOE.

This is a picturesque little town, perched on a hillside, overlooking the Shannon, at a point just below the entrance of Lough Derg. It is one of the chief stations resorted to by large numbers of wandering anglers, who fish the lough in the famous green drake season. There is fair hotel accommodation, and some private lodgings, but when the May-fly carnival is on visitors must not expect too much as the resources of the hostelries are greatly overtaxed. Only one piece of free salmon water is left to the public, out of all that they formerly possessed; and we must, I suppose, be grateful for this small mercy. Here, as elsewhere in Ireland, trout-fishing is free, and the trout are of large size and excellent edible qualities. In the drake season, boats, and capable men to manage them, are scarce, and intending visitors should make their arrangements well in advance. I fished Killaloe from Castle Connell, which is only an easy drive down stream. But this I did because there were three young London anglers at the hotel, two of whom played tin whistles, and the third was great on the banjo. This trio were too exhilarating for a man with nerves, and to avoid the risk of a funeral, I drove to and fro.

Fishing with natural May-fly on Lough Derg is the great attraction which brings to Killaloe a large number of anglers in the spring of the year. A light double-handed trout rod—whole cane, with split cane top—is the correct weapon for this purpose. A fine natural gut cast is tied to a "blow line" of floss silk, about the substance of thick worsted; and this can, with advantage, be spliced on to an ordinary winch line. Two hooks, one an inch above the other, are used, and on these are impaled the live flies. A breeze is necessary to fish successfully, because the gossamer silk line is then blown well in front of the boat. Two men

KILLALOE—ON SHANNON.

From photo by W. Lawrence, Dublin.

can fish together comfortably, one in the stem and the other in the stern, but I set my face against a third rod. The possibilities of hooking monster trout by this daping process, keeps the nerves of the beginner in a state of tension. The great difficulty which all beginners have to overcome is the temptation to strike when the trout rises. So surely as you do, so surely will you miss your fish. These big Derg trout come up with a head and tail rise, like a salmon, and the golden rule is, "Never strike till the tail disappears." It usually takes a day or two of practice before this rule can be uniformly observed, for the boil with which those six-pounders come up is apt to disconcert even experienced English fishermen.

Going out to the fishing ground one morning, we trailed two-inch Devon minnows—one blue and the other silver— and got into a shoal of perch. We crossed and re-crossed their hunting ground, and killed ten or a dozen splendid perch, ranging from $\frac{1}{2}$lb. up to $1\frac{1}{2}$lb. When filleted, and fried in egg and bread crumbs, these fish were delicious. That same evening, on our way home, I mounted a $3\frac{1}{2}$in. gold spoon, using a 14ft. salmon rod, and thus hooked one of the monsters of Lough Derg. For an hour that fish doggedly bored in 15ft. of water, and never moved more than a dozen yards at a time. I could make no greater impression upon this fish than I could upon a submerged tree. It was getting dark; we were two hours late for dinner, and we had a five-mile drive before us. I finally brought matters to a crisis by handing the rod to my chum, taking the line in my hands, as in sea-fishing, and starting to haul that monster to the surface. But he refused to come, struggled violently, and, finally, the thick salmon gut trace snapped! Whatever that fish was—whether salmon or pike—he must have been a leviathan, and my chum will never forgive me for thus recklessly losing him. When lamenting his loss at the landing-stage, an ex-policeman told us he had, the previous season, killed a 20lb. trout in Derg, on a big spoon made out of a shoe-horn. This statement was confirmed subsequently by several credible witnesses who saw the fish weighed.

Another local legend which I heard was a story of the late John Bright and his old fishing crony, Peabody, the philanthropist. They used to fish the Shannon, at Castle Connell, and one day they came up for a turn on the lough. Two of the chief boatmen of Killaloe joined forces, and did themselves the honour of rowing these distinguished visitors. And a severe day's work these rowers had, for their patrons trailed persistently for eight mortal hours, and " never a drop of the cratur had they brought with them " ! Arrived at the landing-stage, late in the evening, there was the inevitable policeman on the bank. John Bright, accosting him, said, "What is the proper price to pay these boatmen, constable?" He replied, "Seven-and-sixpence, your honour; but some gentlemen give them ten shillings." John Bright, turning to his chum, said, "I have no change, Peabody; have you three half-crowns?" The millionaire produced the coins, and gave them to the boatman nearest to him. Holding them in the open palm of one hand, whilst slowly scratching his head with the other, he said, "And they calls ye Paybody, don't they? Well, I calls ye Paynobody."

SHANNON AT KILLALOE.

From photo by W. Lawrence, Dublin.

GALWAY BRIDGE AND SALMON POOL.

From photo. by W. Lawrence, Dublin.

GALWAY AND BALLINAHINCH.

This is one of the best fishing stations in Ireland, not only on account of the sport afforded by the river which runs through the town of Galway itself, but also because of the other waters within easy access. Our illustration of Galway Bridge shows the open water, and the building on the left-hand side of the river as you look towards the bridge is the county prison. Along that bank, beneath the grim, inhospitable shade of the prison walls, is all good fly water, and sometimes it teems with salmon and sea-trout. The bridge itself is a popular fishing station with some anglers, and there was a time when a good deal of snatching used to be done from this position. There is a story told of an angler who, fishing from the bridge, hooked a big retriever dog, and played him up the street in full cry to his owner's house. There the fly was extracted by the aid of a surgeon, and the unfortunate fisherman was soundly abused by the irascible owner of the animal. There is another section of the river, lower down, where £1 a day is charged for the right to fish, and the sport is honestly worth the money if there are fish running. It is very easy fishing, but to those who love rural surroundings, the Galway river will offer few attractions.

With regard to the killing flies, all the Irish patterns kill well, as do many of the Scotch, for fresh-run fish are not very particular.

> "When they will, they will,
> You may depend on't;
> When they won't, they won't,
> And there's an end on't."

I have great faith in plenty of tinsel for fish in tidal water, Silver Doctor, Judge, Dusty Miller, Dunkeld, and Lord Randolph being favourite patterns of mine. But you must not expect your Galway fishermen to admit that such flies are at all suitable for their river. I am unorthodox in this matter of salmon flies, as in a good many other things pertaining to our craft. Salmon are the same in whatever river you find them, be that river in England, Ireland, Scotland, or Wales. The elaborate theories of angling writers on salmon flies have no more solid foundation than have the prejudices of the Galway locals. But it is no part of my present purpose to discuss the salmon fly question; all I will say further on this subject is, if you belong to the noble army of duffers, and know nothing about it, let the locals work their will upon you. If you are an experienced angler, no advice of mine is needed; nor will that of the local quidnuncs have any influence upon you!

There is very good hotel accommodation in Galway, the "Royal" and the "Railway" dividing the business between them; but the latter is my preference. An angling club exists in the town, of which club Mr. R. Townsend is the hon. sec., and through him it is not difficult to get some fishing on a reserved portion of the river. By this I mean, of course, that those who are willing to pay for their sport, can get it at a reasonable price

Lough Corrib is ten miles from Galway, and this lough contains salmon, trout, and pike. For those persons who are fond of lough fishing, Corrib will repay a visit. One of its advantages to the holiday angler is that it fishes best through the latter end of July and the month of August, which is the "dourest" period of the year in most waters. At Oughterard the fisherman will find very good quarters from which he can command the upper and lower Corrib, besides Lake Ross and the Orvonriff river, which is close to the hotel. Corrib boatmen charge 5s. per day, plus the usual lunch and drop of whiskey. The thrifty angler can make his way by mail car to this place, and thence move on to the "Recess" hotel, which commands the Ballinahinch fishing. This car drive will take you, first of all, to Clifden, on your way to Oughterard, and you will see from our illustration of Clifden Falls, what a charming little river is here met with. Unfortunately, this water is let, but there

GALWAY SALMON FISHERY.

From photo by W. Lawrence, Dublin.

CLIFDEN FALL.

From photo by W. Lawrence, Dublin.

is good sea-trout fishing to be had not far away, at Doohulla, and Mr. Maclagan, of Clifden, is the man to apply to for particulars as to terms. There are also several lakes within easy reach of this little town, and of these Lake Ballinaboy is the best, as it contains both sea-trout and salmon, in addition to brown trout and pike. It will thus be seen that this cheap 8s. car ride from Galway to Oughterard, will provide some excellent sport before passing on to that angler's paradise, Ballinahinch. There you have the choice of three hotels, the " Recess," " Anglers," and " Glendalough " —all three good, and all three somewhat expensive; in fact, this is a somewhat costly angler's paradise, in which £12 or £15 per week will be the very lowest sum you may rely upon having to pay, exclusive of drinks. But the fishing is exceedingly good, and it is well worth all the money which it costs. The lowest charge for fishing some of the lakes is 15s. per day, or £3 15s. per week, plus man and boat, and the usual extras. The "Recess" hotel tariff is 10s. 6d. per day for bed and board, and I believe the other hotels charge the same. As will be seen by our illustration of the Ballinahinch river, it is a pretty piece of fly-water, but it is not of any great extent, the run from the lough to the sea being only four Irish miles. This stream flows through an exceedingly wild and picturesque district, which cannot fail to impress the English visitor with a sense of waste and desolation.

In addition to the four miles of river, the fishing extends through a chain of loughs, extending for a distance of sixteen miles. There is a limit of twenty-one rods on the best length of the fishing, and intending visitors would do well to write to Mr. Blackadder, the manager of the Ballinahinch fisheries, and ascertain particulars.

The sea-trout fishing in these loughs is real good sport, especially as it is no uncommon thing to rise a salmon to your trout flies; but I do not care much for lough-fishing. The monotony of the thing palls upon me, no matter how good the sport may be, after a few hours. One of the many points in favour of this place is the fact that you can fish it, with the certainty of getting sport, at any part of the season, from start to finish. And the secret of the splendid scores made both upon the river and lakes of Ballinahinch is to be found in the fact that the salmon and sea-trout have a free run up from the sea. No nets, no traps, no weirs—"no nothing"—to impede their upward passage, except the fly of the angler. As a consequence, there is always a splendid stock of salmon and sea-trout in the water, and it is not too much to say that the sea-trout fishing to be obtained here can only be beaten in one place within the United Kingdom. Where that other place is, neither rack nor thumb-screw should wring from me the name!

WESTPORT, CO. MAYO.

A good many visitors to Ballina, and other fishing stations in Co. Mayo, pay a visit to Westport, which is within a short railway journey of Loughs Conn and Cullen. There is plenty of free trout fishing to be had at Westport, where the river shown in our illustration empties itself into Clew Bay. But Lord Sligo owns the best of the water, and the wandering angler must rely upon the Erriff for salmon and sea trout, for which tickets at reasonable charges are to be had for the asking.

I fished at Westport after finishing a fortnight's Mayfly work, on the Westmeath lakes, and the relief of wandering on a river's bank, after being penned up in a boat, was very delightful. I should not at all object to put in an angling holiday at Westport, and it is especially worthy the attention of that large class of anglers, whose love of the sport is greater than their pecuniary resources.

BALLINAHINCH.

From photo by W. Lawrence, Dublin.

WESTPORT—BELCLARE SALMON LEAP.

From photo by W. Lawrence, Dublin.

THE ITCHEN.

There are many worse ways of spending an angling holiday than by putting in a week on the Itchen. Even a couple of days are not to be despised, if you cannot manage a longer time. Winchester is within easy reach of town, and the fishing in this old cathedral city is, as a consequence, much sought after. The lengths of the "old barge" river and the mill-stream, shown in our illustration, are fishable by half-crown day tickets, and I have had some very fair sport on them both, in the month of May, and also later in the season. One late evening rise upon the mill-stream will long linger in my memory, because I had some good fun in the twilight, and basketed several capital fish. The day had been exceedingly hot and sultry, and the trout were too lazy even to wag their tails. I had mooned the day away, hunting the ditches in the water meadows, and saving myself up for the evening. This is a practice which I strongly recommend to other brothers of the craft, because there is many a man who leaves off, weary and disgusted, at the very time when the fish come on to feed. Well, I had put in a thoroughly idle day, and, when the sun went down, I was as "fresh as paint and keen as mustard."

But here let me turn aside, and beguile the time until the trout come on, by some discursive remarks upon evening rises in general. They are uncertain things to save yourself up for, because the more cocksure you are about getting a "mad" rise, the more likely are you to find the river perfectly dead, and not a fin moving! I am very often tempted to ask, are the habits of our chalk-stream trout changing, or is their indifference to an evening meal of surface-food due to abominable north and easterly winds? Whatever the cause, the fact remains that those of us who catch last trains home, and even go to roost in village hostelries for the sake of the evening rises, get little or nothing to repay us for our sacrifices and perseverance. The months of July and August are essentially the periods during which chalk-stream trout were wont to indulge in at least a fool's half hour each evening; and what scores some of us have made in times past, whilst these brief, mad rises have been on! But what has now come over the fish? For the two past seasons I have failed to meet with one single good evening rise, though I fish incessantly; and this year of grace bids fair to be the worst that we South of England men have known—in this connection—during the past quarter of a century. A marked reduction in the number of nocturnal fly may explain the decline of this branch of sport to some extent, the falling-off in the supply of sedges, caperers, silverhorns, and other luscious water-bred flies of kindred varieties being most marked. In their place we have those minute aphides, the tiny fisherman's curse, which are the inevitable accompaniment of a chilly evening with a nor'-easterly wind succeeding a hot day. Not only do we get these wee pests in place of the big flies, after which the big trout were wont to souse and flounder, with a reckless disregard of personal safety, which frequently gave us four or five brace of good fish in the last hour of daylight, but no sooner does the sun now disappear, than up comes the river fog—and fishing is henceforth a waste of labour. We are a grumbling set, no doubt; and that we never are but always to be blessed is an orthodox tenet of our creed; but I do protest that we dry-fly men have been sorely tried during the past two or three seasons. Time was when, in the months of July and August, I was accustomed to make good baskets of fish, unfailingly, when the sun had disappeared, but these record scores are a thing of the past, and a brace of good trout are now counted as phenomenal results of an evening rise. And now, after that grumble, we went back to the "Old Barge," and tried our luck with a red-quill gnat. Nothing but small fish were rising, apparently, and some half-dozen eight-inch trout had to be put back. When the monotony of this kind

WINCHESTER—THE OLD BARGE.

From photo by A. G. Eder, Winchester.

of thing began to pall upon us, and it was getting dusk, we repaired to the mill-stream, by the footpath. The water was low, but the trout were on the go along the sides, sometimes grubbing about with their back fins out of water. I mounted a grey gnat, with a flat silver body and badger legs, and those trout took it greedily. I made a basket of four brace of fish before it became quite dark, and I took the last brace quite close up to the stile shown in our illustration.

And the next day was a red-letter day with me, for I fished some distance above Winchester, and started by falling into one of the dykes which are used for irrigating purposes. But this soaking did not matter much, because it rained incessantly the whole mortal day, and we were plodding through long grass up to our thighs. Yes, it was what my Welsh friends call a "nice soft day," but the trout took the sunk alder madly! No wonder Kingsley wrote a prose poem on this fly, if the Itchen trout take it in that fashion. I paid ten shillings for my day's fishing, and I had 14lb. of trout for my money, including a couple of two-pounders.

In some lengths of this river, which I am accustomed to fish, the grayling have crowded out the trout. But "Thymallus" has a strong disinclination to rise to a floating fly, and of those fish which show upon the shallows, very few, except the small ones, have been taking surface food. This is, no doubt, due to the extraordinary scarcity of natural fly, which has prevailed throughout the whole season. In one of the lower lengths of the Itchen, the other day, I fished over any number of big grayling that were rooting amongst the weeds, and nothing in the shape of a fly would they look at, either wet or dry. In this piece of water "Thymallus" has increased and multiplied to such an enormous extent that they bid fair to exterminate the trout—and yet it has been impossible to kill anything like a basket of fish upon the fly. "Keep all you catch, regardless of size," said my host. "We want to reduce their numbers." I did as he requested, and I was not at all proud of the results of a long day's fishing. It is true that, by casting up-stream and allowing the fly to sink, I did get hold of a few fish, but only two good ones took my sunk fly, and both of these got off, after a brief skittering fight. The expert trout fisherman has much to learn before he can attain to anything like proficiency in the art of catching grayling. Of course, I refer only to those streams where nothing but the fly is permitted to be used, but judging by the "side" put on by successful "floaters of the worm," I suppose that my statement holds good in regard to that unclean method of capture. The worm has no charm for me, and those who use it are welcome to all the fish they catch—I would prefer to go home with an empty creel. This may be Quixotic, southern prejudice, but I plead guilty to it, and am not ashamed to do so. Foregathering with a man, the other day, by the riverside, on a length of the Itchen teeming with grayling, I asked him, "What has been your best basket this season?" He lifted the lid of his creel, and said, "There it is!" The contents consisted of a brace, the best $1\frac{3}{4}$lb., and the other $1\frac{1}{4}$lb. And this man had fished two or three days a week upon one of the best lengths of the Itchen all through the season! Verily we anglers are a patient and long-suffering class of the community, and it takes but little in the shape of tangible results to repay us for our expenditure of toil and money! But does the contents of the creel represent our only return? No! A day by the riverside takes us out of ourselves; the world and all its petty vexations slide away from us as we cast the fly, and the brain-worker gains more from a few hours thus spent than he would from any other source of recreation.

THE ITCHEN—LORD NORTHBROOK'S FISHERY.

From photo by A. G. Bishop, Winchester.

CANTERBURY STOUR—LOWER FISHERY.

Photo by C. Neslott, Canterbury.

THE CANTERBURY STOUR.

The Lower Stour, below our Kent Cathedral city, is shown in an accompanying illustration and from this it will be seen what a pretty trout stream the Stour is in places. Thanks to the long sustained efforts of Mr. F. C. Nash, the hon. sec. of an angling club, the preservation and constant restocking of this water has greatly improved the sport of subscribers during the past few seasons. Pike were formerly a source of much vexation and loss, but persistent efforts have well nigh exterminated them. The Falstaff Hotel, at Canterbury, is the nearest and most conveniently situated house for those fishing the Lower Stour, and I can speak well of this famous old hostelry. The trout season opens on April 1st and closes September 30th, and the price of a season ticket is only four guineas. All the funds of the club are expended in artificially hatching and rearing of trout and the care of the river. There are some very deep holes in the lower reaches, wherein pike, perch, tench, and roach are caught by bottom fishermen, and daily tickets at 1s. each are issued for this class of angling. There is also an angling club lower down, whose water extends from Fordwich to Stourmouth, and the season tickets for this length cost a guinea.

Above the town, from Canterbury to Shalmsford, is an excellent piece of association water, upon which it is possible occasionally to find a vacancy for a rod on reasonable terms. The Stour is a typical slow-running, chalk sream, where no one but a professor of the dry-fly art stands any chance of scoring. All the flies enumerated for Darenth fishing kill equally well on this Canterbury river, and all the local fishermen here swear by the dressings of Mr. G. Holland, of Winchester. Some people say that catching trout does not depend so much upon the fly as upon the man who drives it. There is a grain of truth in this saying, but none the less, George Holland's flies add greatly to the chances of success, and his productions will take a lot of beating. For some time there was a strong prejudice against double-winged flies, but no one who has tried them once would go back to single wings again. The Stour above the town of Canterbury produces May-fly, and good sport is there to be had with it, but this fly does not breed in the lower water. I can remember when the same condition of things existed upon the Darenth, when no May-fly bred below Eynsford viaduct. But there was a wholesale cutting of weeds in the middle of the May-fly season, and those weeds carried down with them a supply of "Mays" which stocked four or five miles of river in which they had never been seen before. I mention this as an encouragement to Mr. F. C. Nash, and other friends, who are endeavouring to establish a May-fly hatchery in the Lower Stour fishery.

ANGLING HOLIDAYS IN SCOTLAND.

The land o' cakes is essentially the happy hunting ground of well-to-do Englishmen, and as there is a fashion in holiday-making, as in everything else, it is considered the correct thing to go to Scotland. And what grand fishing is there to be got, if only your purse is long enough to enable you to obtain it! The new line of railway through the Highlands has greatly cheapened the cost of travel to many of the most beautiful angling resorts, and, what is equally important to a good many men, is the enormous saving of time thus effected. In the limited space left at my disposal I can, in the present volume, do little more than touch briefly upon a few of the angling holiday resorts that are open to the wandering fisherman. Taking these fishing stations in the order in which they will be met with in a railway journey through the Highlands, our first halting place is Tarbet. Here we strike Lough Lomond.

HEAD OF LOCH LOMOND.

HEAD OF LOCH LOMOND.

Lomond is an enormous sheet of water, some twenty odd miles long and its principal feeder is the Arklet, whose famous falls are one of Scotland's many "sights." A steamer, the "Lady of the Lake," will enable fishermen to vary their location in search of trout, and they will do well, in times of rain fall, to cultivate the many brooks and burns with which the whole of this watershed is intersected. There is excellent hotel accommodation at various points about the loch, "Inversnaid" and "Ardlin" commanding one end, "Tarbet" and "Howardenwan" opposite sides in mid-distance, whilst "Luss" is the spot for cruising about the islands, and "Balloch" for the lower extremity. Before leaving Tarbet do not omit to pay a visit to Loch Long and the stream connecting it with Lomond. All the ordinary Scotch flies kill well in these Highland lakes, and the visitor cannot do better than put himself into the hands of Mr. W. J. Cummins, of Bishop Auckland, who will set him up with an assortment of the best patterns.

Within easy reach of the Inversnaid Hotel are several famous sheets of water, which are now made accessible, and of these the next in order is Loch Katrine.

LOCH KATRINE.

The fishing in this beautiful loch is limited to trout, which is free, the charge for boat and man being 5s. per day. The Trossachs Hotel is the best house to command this queen of Scottish lakes; also lochs Achray and Vennachar. There are no boats upon the last-named water. There is another little lake, connected by a stream with Vennachar, which will well repay the trouble of getting at it. I refer to Drunkie, which contains remarkably good trout, both in size and quality.

As to the natural beauties of Katrine, it would be impossible for me to do them justice; but, by common consent, this loch is admitted to have no equal in the United Kingdom.

LOCH LEVEN, ARGYLESHIRE.

The wandering angler has had this district opened up to him by the Highland Railway, which lands him at Fort William. From thence he can go, by steamer, to Ballachulish, and do the rest of the journey by coach. The drive through the famous Glen of Coe—following the course of the river of that name—affords one of the finest sights in Scotland. For rugged grandeur and sublime solitude there is nothing equal to it in the United Kingdom. The river Coe receives the rainfall of the mountains which environ this famous pass of Glencoe, and thus forms the main feeder of the Argyleshire Loch Leven. The Coe is also the breeding ground of the Leven trout, who head up this stream, and there afford good sport to the few anglers who visit it. In the journey through the glen, comfortable quarters will be found at various stages, with a modest tariff and free trouting, amidst the wildest of nature's solitudes. For a jaded man, seeking mental rest, combined with good Scotch trout fishing, the angling holiday-seeker will not make a mistake who goes to the Argyleshire Loch Leven. But he must not aspire to do anything heroic, in the way of slaughtering big fish, nor must he expect to have his deeds recorded

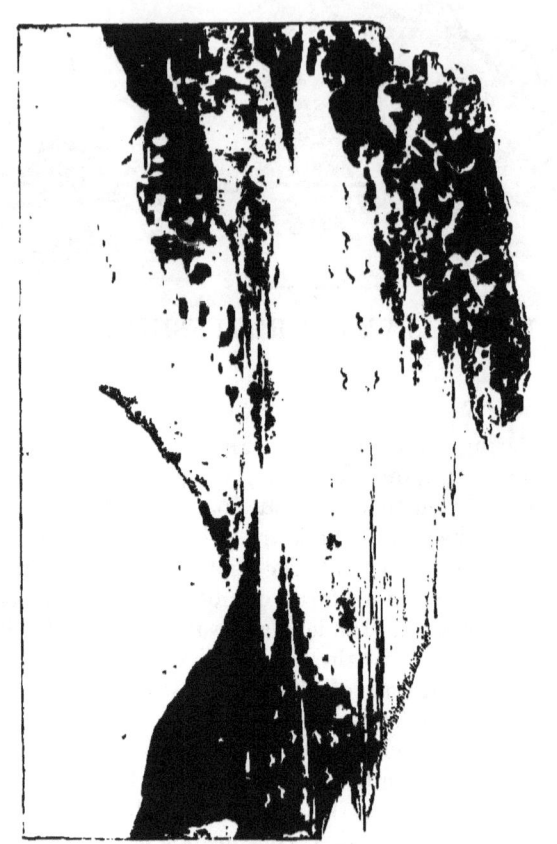

LOCH LEVEN, AND PASS OF GLENCOE.

in the sporting papers, as the doings of a mighty hunter in the sight of our Lord. If he is just content to appreciate the sport of killing good baskets of medium-sized trout, and enjoying the homely comforts of roadside inns, in which he will be treated as one of the family, then let him go to this out-of-the-way corner of Scotland. The

THE LOCH IN GLENCOE.

coming and going of the daily coach-load of visitors will not interfere with his sport, and if these scurrying tourists do look upon him as a harmless lunatic—wasting his time after trout, instead of "doing" Scotland—he can well afford to accept their sympathy in a becoming spirit of humility.

The loch itself is a very fine sheet of water, of considerable extent, and the stream fishing is everywhere excellent in this little fished watershed. From Ballachulish the coach drive through the glen extends to a distance of thirty miles, and all this is over historical ground, for is it not the home of the once mighty clan of the Macdonalds?

The angler will do well to break his journey at various stages, where accommodation is obtainable, commencing at the entrance of the glen, where there is a very comfortable little hotel, and then following the course of the river through the sublime solitudes of this beautiful glen. There is a capital hotel—the King's House—at the further end of the pass, and there is excellent trout fishing close at hand.

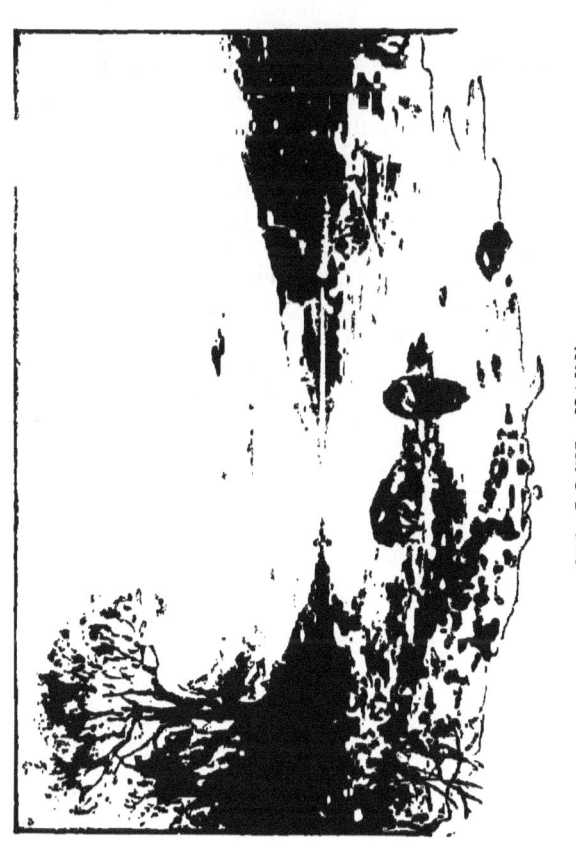

ON LOCH EARN

ON LOCH ERNE.

The best quarters for commanding these waters is the Drummond Arms, at St. Fillans, where the fishing upon both the loch and the streams which feed it is all free. The outflow from Erne finds its way into the Firth of Tay, and gathering from feeders on its way becomes a considerable stream lower down. Within easy distance of St. Fillans, there is plenty of trout fishing to be had in all directions, and the surroundings are exceedingly beautiful.

At no great distance the wandering angler can pass on to Loch Tay, and there try his luck for a 20lb. salmon. The Killin Hotel, where the charges for bed and board are 10s. per day, and the cost of boat and man 4s. per day, plus the usual lunch, trout fishing is free to persons staying at the Killin or Kenmore hotels.

LOCH TAY.

The Kenmore end of the loch—for three miles—is reserved for salmon, by Lord Breadalbane, but trout fishing is free over the whole lake. This reservation makes it advisable for the would-be-salmon-catcher to take up his residence with host Maisey, of the Killin Hotel, at the upper end of the water. No doubt the lower end is much the best in the early part of the season, when fresh-run fish come up the famous River Tay into the loch; but the upper water yields a good many splendid fish to visitors who troll for them. When I say "fish," of course I mean salmon. No one, with the slightest pretensions to be considered a sportsman would call a trout a fish; and as for a pike, well, he is just a pike, and nothing more! Phantom and Devon minnows, spoons of silver and spoons of gold—copper and brass—are amongst the tempting lures with which the Tay salmon are here beguiled by the angling holiday-makers. But it is a nice, lazy way of spending a few days, if you belong to the noble army of angling duffers, in trolling upon Loch Tay. A chum of mine, who had never caught a fish of any kind in his life, was some three years ago beguiled into a boat from the Killin end of the Tay. A rod was put into his hands, with instructions to do nothing with it except prevent its falling overboard. Trailing a minnow around the shallows he caught several pike, and this excited him so much that he was threatened with expulsion from the boat if he did not restrain himself.

It is a curious fact that whenever I have gone out on a loch with a man who knows little or nothing of fishing he invariably has all the best of the luck. And so my friend, on this occasion, had no sooner been reproved for his boisterous hilarity than "whizz"! went his salmon reel, and a grand fish flung himself out of the water forty yards astern of the boat. And now it was our turn to score off our hitherto jubilant chum. He implored us to take the rod and kill that fish, but we would have nothing to do with it. "Keep your rod top up, and leave the winch alone," was our first piece of advice, and presently our duffer cooled down and did exactly as he was told, until at last he brought his fish to gaff, and then sank, trembling with excitement, into the stern sheets of the boat. It was a grand thick fish of $19\frac{1}{2}$lbs., very short and deep for its weight, and to say that my friend was proud of his capture is to do less than justice to the facts. As a matter of fact, that salmon marks an epoch in his life—some of his cronies say it has been the ruin of him—but, at any rate, he has been badly crazed on fishing ever since.

Perhaps I ought to mention the fact that there is a charge of £1 5s. per day for salmon fishing, or 30s. per day for two persons occupying the same boat. Weekly tickets for salmon, £5. As this is a district much affected by holiday-seekers, other than anglers, and as the number of boats are limited, the wandering fisherman would do well to bespeak both bed and boat in advance.

Above Killin, and running into the loch there, is the River Dochart, which forms a connecting link between Lochs Awe and Tay.

RIVER DOCHART, KILLIN.

The Dochart, as will be seen from our illustration, is an ideal fly stream, and there is no difficulty about getting permission to fish it. The landlord of the Royal Hotel can put you right about the matter, because he always has a length of the river at his disposal.

Following the course of the Dochart, we thus reach Loch Awe, the distance between Tay and Awe being about 20 miles.

LOCH AWE.

This is a splendid all-round fishing loch—some 25 miles long—containing salmon, brown trout, sea-trout, ferox, pike, and perch, and the whole of the fishing is free. Dalmally is the uppermost station, at the head of the loch, but there is no lack of fishing quarters. Amongst the favourite anglers' quarters in this district is Taynuilt,, Port Sonachan, Ford, and some others; but the last-named is one of the best for sport.

THE ORCHY.

At the Dalmally end of Loch Awe the river Orchy winds through a very pretty glen, and a glance at the accompanying illustration will show what an attractive stream this is to the fly fisherman. Personally, I would rather have one day's fishing on the Orchy, when in good tune, than a week on Loch Awe, or any other lake, for the matter of that. The Orchy is the main feeder which supplies Loch Awe, and it is a good salmon river.

PASS OF BRANDER—LOCH AWE.

Another favourite spot where fishing from the shore can be indulged in is the Pass of Brander, and the advantage of having such alternatives to the loch will be manifest to all experienced anglers.

LOCH LEVEN—KINROSS.

From Loch Awe to Kinross is a far cry, but I cannot omit to mention this famous trout lake, which is situated 17 miles from Perth. It is, undoubtedly, the best lough fishing in Scotland, and so it ought to be, in view of the fact that the charge for fishing and boatmen is 3s. per hour, plus 3s. 6d. for their lunch, including a pint of whiskey and two quarts of beer! And to this it is expected that you will add a tip of 1s. per day to each of your two men. The hotel charges are on the same liberal scale, and Leven, therefore, ranks amongst the most expensive, as well as the best, loch trout fishing in the United Kingdom. This fishing is run by a company, and there is small wonder that they pay fat dividends.

The Loch Leven trout are free risers and bold fighters, and in appearance they are quite different to the ordinary brown trout, being longer and thinner, and more silvery in colour. It is usual to see it stated that the fish taken in this loch average 1lb. each, but such is not the case, according to my experience. If you allow ¾lb. as an average, that would be nearer the mark, but even at that figure a basket of such fish make a very handsome show as the result of a day's fishing.

It is not given to all of us to be content to pay 30s. per day for trout fishing, and I, personally, prefer something a little less heroic. The bare charges at Green's hotel, including fishing, amount to £2 6s. 6d. per day.

Except in rough weather, when there is a big ripple on, the use of large flies is a mistake. Fine fishing pays quite as well in Loch Leven as it does everywhere else. The man who uses single X-drawn gut at point, and finest natural for the remainder of the cast, will rise far more fish than those who use coarse casts. The same remark applies to the size of flies; the most successful Leven anglers in calm water are those who fish the smallest patterns.

THE END.

HARDY'S GOLD MEDAL RODS

As made for the late H.R.H. Prince Albert Victor and leading Sportsmen.

CANE BUILT WITH AND WITHOUT STEEL CENTRES, AND GREENHEART FOR SALMON, TROUT, GRAYLING, MAHSEER, &c.

ARE BEYOND COMPETITION.

The "FIELD":—"It is to Messrs. Hardy, of Alnwick, we owe the supremacy we have achieved as rod makers."

33 PRIZE MEDALS, &c., &c.
The Largest Number held by any House in the World.

The GOLD MEDAL "FISHERIES" EXHIBITION, LONDON 1883.
Only PRIZE MEDAL "INVENTIONS" EXHIBITION, LONDON, 1885.
Only GOLD MEDAL, Liverpool, 1886. Only PRIZE MEDAL, Newcastle-on-Tyne, 1887 1889, Awards PARIS and COLOGNE, etc., etc.
Only Makers of "H. C. Pennell's," "H. S. Hall's," "Marston," "Kelson," "Hi Regan," "Red Spinner," and "Major Turle's" Patterns.
The "PERFECTION," "GEM," "BADMINTON," the "PERFECT TEST" ROD, "HOUGHTON," "PRINCESS," and the celebrated "ALNWICK," "GREENHEART," and "HOTSPUR" RODS.

SPECIALITIES

FOR

Salmon Fishing.
Trout Fishing.
Pike Fishing.
Roach Fishing.
Sea Fishing.
Lake Fishing.
River Fishing.

IMPORTANT.

If you want the best of everything in

Fishing Rods and Tackle,

for any part of the world, write us, it will pay you.

Remember the "BEST" is always the cheapest.

HARDY'S CATALOGUE,
260 Pages, FREE SEND ADDRESS.

Over 260 pages, with 300 Illustrations, is bristling with their latest Practical Inventions in Salmon, Trout, Pike, Barbel, Roach, etc., Rods, Reels, Reel Fittings, Lines, Line Dryer, "Harpoon" Salmon Fly Hooks, Pneumatic Cushion Button for Salmon Rods, New "Halcyon" Spinners, "Hog-backed Flying Bar Spoons," "Amber" and "Pennell" Devons, Sea Rods, Reels, Tackle, etc. Original articles giving practical hints on almost every class of Angling; also information regarding the Choice of Rods, Reels, Nets, etc., with fifteen Recipes for Cooking Trout.

HARDY BROTHERS, London & North British Works,
ALNWICK, ENGLAND.

RETAIL BRANCHES { 5, SOUTH ST. DAVID STREET, EDINBURGH.
{ 12 & 14, MOULT STREET, MANCHESTER.

LAKE VYRNWY HOTEL.   **N. WALES, VIA OSWESTRY.**
Nearest Station, Llanfyllin, Cambrian Railway. LAKE VYRNWY covers 1,100 acres; 650 reserved for fly only. The Loch Leven of Wales—trout only.   Apply, MISS DAVIES, as above.

GEORGE HOLLAND,

29, The Square, WINCHESTER,

is Exhibiting at the Royal Aquarium

HOLLAND'S FLOATING FLIES.
HOLLAND'S COBWEB GUT.
HOLLAND'S DRY-FLY RODS.

Warranted to catch Eels in Pond, River, or Stream. Highest Awards for Traps — Bronze Medal and Diploma, Truro, 1893; Silver Medal and Diploma, Scarborough, 1895. "Glanusk Park, Crick Lowell, July 23, 1895. The two Eel Traps you sent to Sir Joseph Bailey have been most successful; we caught 68 Eels yesterday morning. — HUBERT C. BAILEY." "Bridport, August 28, 1895.—The Eel Trap answers very well indeed; we caught upwards of 30 Eels last night the first time we put it in.—Yours truly, JOHN FOWLER." "H.M. Prison, Canterbury,—The Eel Trap I had in the Spring has proved itself equal to three of the wicker ones I was using.—W. H. OXLEY." *Price Lists and full particulars free.* Address: A. CLIFFORD, Patent Works, Hawley, Kent.

W. J. CUMMINS,

PRACTICAL ANGLER

AND MANUFACTURER OF

RODS, REELS, LINES, FLIES,

AND

Every requisite for Salmon, Trout and Grayling.

It will well repay Anglers to write for Catalogue before placing Orders.

MERCERS' ARMS HOTEL, KILREA.

ROBERT KIRK, Proprietor.

www.ingramcontent.com/pod-product-compliance
Lightning Source LLC
Chambersburg PA
CBHW032147230426
43672CB00011B/2472